George Clinton Densmore Odell

Simile and Metaphor in the English and Scottish Ballads

George Clinton Densmore Odell

Simile and Metaphor in the English and Scottish Ballads

ISBN/EAN: 9783744766357

Printed in Europe, USA, Canada, Australia, Japan

Cover: Foto ©Thomas Meinert / pixelio.de

More available books at **www.hansebooks.com**

SIMILE AND METAPHOR

IN THE

ENGLISH AND SCOTTISH BALLADS

BY

GEORGE CLINTON DENSMORE ODELL, A.M.
COLUMBIA COLLEGE, 1890

DISSERTATION SUBMITTED IN PARTIAL FULFILMENT OF THE REQUIRE-
MENTS FOR THE DEGREE OF DOCTOR OF PHILOSOPHY IN
THE UNIVERSITY FACULTY OF PHILOSOPHY,
COLUMBIA COLLEGE

NEW YORK
1892

PREFATORY NOTE.

The edition of the ballads used in the preparation of this essay is the well-known collection of Professor Francis J. Child, of Harvard University. This collection, entitled "English and Scottish Popular Ballads," was published in Boston in 1857–58, and contains in its eight generous volumes all the material needed for a paper of the present scope. The early edition of Professor Child, for various reasons, was used in preference to the new and somewhat larger edition which is just completed and which will surely become the abiding monument of ballad literature. In the first place, the new edition was unfinished until the bulk of the essay was in final form, and, more important still, that edition with its complicated system of including all ballads of the same nature under one general head paved the way to certain difficulties which, in the matter of reference, would inevitably lead to confusion. In view of this fact, it seemed permissible to use the older yet by no means unsatisfactory edition of 1857–58. The ballads in this early collection taken from Percy's Reliques, I have carefully collated with the reprint of the Percy Folio MS., and none of the learned bishop's interpolations have been allowed to stand among the figures quoted in the essay. The titles of the ballads mentioned in the text that follows, except in the few cases where specific reference is made to the Percy Folio MS., are given as they occur in the older Child edition, and the figures appended to the title in each instance refer, respectively, to the line of the poem, and the volume and the page of that edition.

The various ballad collections of Percy, Ritson, Scott, Motherwell, Aytoun, etc., as well as the numerous magazine articles on this favourite topic have been examined, and whatever could throw light on puzzling questions has been freely borrowed from such sources. The indebtedness will be so very apparent to all lovers of poetry that it may pass with the acknowledgment here given; for without the labours of these patient collectors, English literature would still lack what has proved to be one of its most interesting and fruitful branches.

SIMILE AND METAPHOR

IN THE

ENGLISH AND SCOTTISH BALLADS.

THE PURPOSE OF THE ESSAY.

The amount of criticism that has been bestowed on the English and Scotch popular songs is already so great that some apology seems necessary by way of prelude to a new essay. These songs have been treated in many ways and from many points of view. Critics have disputed concerning their origin, and antiquarians have battled over the question of their age; students of language have broken lances over the authenticity of particular ballads, and riming *dilettanti* have blandly deceived the world with the product of their own brains. All these questions, however, have now been settled as definitely as the somewhat uncertain nature of the evidence will allow, and it remains for the future writer to glean his harvest from new or half-neglected fields. The ballads are always fresh, but much of the ballad discussion is already dry to the taste.

While various attempts have been made to define the true ballad style, it has occurred to no one, apparently, to appeal to the trial by figure. In other words, no effort has been put forth to show what figures are most common in the popular verse and what figures, therefore, were, and are, most intelligible to the popular mind and most beloved of the popular heart. This question seems to throw open a most fruitful field of inquiry, and to it the following pages owe their origin. The results of such an investigation, far from being meagre, as might be surmised, are singularly rich and convincing, and they are given here in the hope that they may stimulate further study in the same direction.

The object in so dealing with ballad literature must be evident to all; for if the figures found in these songs are sufficiently alike to be placed in one general group, two things will be proved most conclusively. In the first place we shall see by what means the British mind, unaided, perhaps, or it may be from inherited Indo-Germanic tradition, has worked its way to the utilising of resemblances as helps to thought; and in the second place, we will have a clue to the authenticity of any ballad, intangible to the novice, yet to the student unanswerable as any proof that may be brought forward. For if the popular mind uses one kind of figure, and an alleged popular song one that is radically different, we shall have reason to doubt the genuineness of the song. It is the object of this essay, by supplying a firm and substantial groundwork for such study, to further investigation on similar lines in the English, and thence perhaps in the ballad literature of other nations.

THE ORIGIN AND NATURE OF BALLAD LITERATURE.

The reason for the foregoing statements will appear after a brief outline of the history of the ballad. It will be seen that this essay, dealing with only one branch—and that a limited one—of the ballad question, is but remotely concerned with the origin of the songs; yet some idea of the ballads themselves seems not only desirable, but essential, for a complete understanding of the subject. From the time when in 1765, Percy published his "Reliques of Ancient English Poetry," the amount of writing on the characteristics of these homely productions has been enormous, and in many cases, highly instructive. At any rate, it has been edifying to the writers themselves, and has served to arouse and hold public interest to a degree little short of phenomenal.

The ballads of a country may be described, briefly, as the unpremeditated outpouring of the national heart. They put into convenient phrase the popular idea of life in its various relations. For the sake of emphasis, the idea is moulded in the form of a story; as in all true poetry, it is the concrete expression of what in the abstract would be unintelligible to the popular mind. Hence, instead of inculcating lessons in virtue, the ballad relates a harrowing tale of the consequences of vice. This much at least may be confidently affirmed : a ballad, whoever its author may be, must reflect the life and thought of the time and place ; otherwise, it ceases to be a ballad, and, whatever its merits, is but the work of an individual, striving to express his own views on the world about him. The true balladist, in other words, merges his identity in the mass of the people, and becomes, as it were, but the mouthpiece of his generation. The authorship of a ballad is, in this sense, as completely national as if it were a mosaic in words, every element of which has come from a different source in what we are pleased to call, collectively, the popular intelligence.

Concerning the origin of the ballads, various theories are maintained. Percy in his admirable essay prefixed to the Reliques, gives the minstrels as the authors of the popular song. "The minstrels," he affirms, "were an order of men in the middle ages, who subsisted by the arts of poetry and music and sang to the harp verses composed by themselves. They also appear to have accompanied their songs with mimicry and action ; and to have practised such various means of diverting as were much admired in those rude times, and supplied the want of more refined entertainment." This passage was violently criticised by Ritson, who sought to degrade the minstrel profession as much as Percy had laboured to elevate it ; and Percy, "wedded to no hypothesis," changed, in the fourth edition of his work, the disputed sentence to "composed by themselves *or others*."

Whatever may have been the authorship of the old ballads, they seem certainly to have been sung in very early times by the gleemen—afterwards minstrels. Anglo-Saxon poetry, to which Percy and Ritson seem to have made no recourse, proves the existence of minstrels from the beginning of what may be called English history in England. At any rate, Mr. Aytoun, one of the latest and best critics in this field, regards the ballads as the work of Ritson's despised minstrels. Speaking of the ballads, "their number," he says, "as we have them now, without attempting to estimate the many which must have disappeared in the course of time, is a clear proof that they were not composed casually or from the caprice of writers, but were the production of minstrels, who in remoter times, followed their craft as a regular profession or means of livelihood. . . . At the courts of our earlier Scottish kings, and at the mansions of the principal nobility . . . minstrelsy was a favourite pastime. . . . And the minstrel, wherever he went, be it to castle or cottage, received a ready or most hospitable welcome." * His song, besides, paid for food and lodging.

And again :

"I tender them [the foregoing remarks] as an explanation of the origin of the ballads, which I do not regard as mere casual compositions, dictated by the fancy of individuals who had a natural taste for poetry, or an ambition for making themselves known as men of superior capacity in a small or obscure circle, but as *professional works*, undertaken both for livelihood and fame, which must ever have some connection." *

After the degradation of the minstrels from their high position, which happened, no doubt, toward the close of the age of chivalry, these guardians of the ancient song travelled from place to place, each probably having his own circuit, singing and amusing the common people with their lays. Mr. Dixon, in his valuable prefaces, writes of the last of these minstrels still lingering (1845-1846) in the north of England and in Scotland. Their songs were handed down from age to age and became the most precious possession of the people. Sung in these times to the rude and wondering peasantry, it was by the peasantry, after the race of minstrels became almost extinct, that the songs were preserved for many years, and it is, in fact, due to the labours of antiquarians like Scott and Motherwell, in gathering these remains of minstrelsy from the recitation of often ignorant peasants, that we owe the imposing array of ballad poetry that to-day enriches English literature. The ballads taken down from the recitation of Mrs. Brown of Falk-

* Introduction to The Ballads of Scotland.

land are among the finest specimens of popular song extant in any language; not that this lady, however, is to be classed among the ignorant reciters above mentioned.

So much may be said for the origin of the ballads. They have been preserved by oral tradition, and such changes as have occurred are verbal, and consist of the substitution of modern for archaic phraseology. Maintaining such a fight against oblivion, never printed, indeed regarded, frequently, as the property of individual minstrels,* it is not strange that the handling of illiterate bards and the crooning of old women on the hillside and by the fireside have tended to mutilate the original form of the poems. Hence arise the different versions of particular songs, the best possible proof of their authenticity.

The day of popular song, however, is past; the printing press sounded its death-knell. "The process of national ballad growing and ballad preserving can only go on while those concerned in the process are unconscious of the presence of an outer world with an eye fixed upon it. The moment it is discovered, and public attention drawn to it, it stops. . . . The time will shortly be, if it has not yet come, when the oldest woman in the country will only be able to repeat to you 'Gil Morice' or 'Sir Patrick Spens' from some printed version." †

And yet, though the authorship is national, if the phrase may be allowed, although, as the same learned critic † asserts, "it knows no authorship but that of the country at large," and is "truly autochthonous," the stories will often be found to be of almost Indo-Germanic currency. To cite one instance alone, Professor Child traces the well-known ballad whose numerous versions he classes under the title of "Lady Isabel and the Elf-Knight," to English, Dutch, Danish, Swedish, Norwegian, German, Polish, French, Italian, Spanish, Portuguese, and Magyar relationship: surely, a sufficiently imposing array of connexions for any ballad.

Enough has been said to shew that these songs arose from the people, for the people, and were preserved lovingly and carefully, by the people.

* Aytoun, Introduction to The Ballads of Scotland, 4th Ed., p. xliii.
† Blackwood, page 465, Oct., 1858.

Of the nature of the ballads, one may write with more certainty. They may be divided roughly under four heads:

(1.) Historical Ballads—dealing with national warfare or private feud;
(2.) Ballads of the Affections—including poems of love and sorrow;
(3.) Ballads of Superstition—including those that deal with ghosts and fairy-lore; and
(4.) Humorous Ballads—on particular political crises, and also including a number of popular riddles.

The ballads that are unquestionably genuine show the same traits of simplicity and directness. They begin immediately on the story, without a word of introduction, as in "Sir Patrick Spens,"

> " The King sits in Dunfermline toun,
>   Drinking the blude-red wine;
> ' O whaur shall I get a skeely skipper,
>   To sail this ship of mine?' "

The language is plain and to the point, but full of homely strength and pathos; as Motherwell says, "there is no pause made on the way for beautiful images or appropriate illustrations. If these come naturally and unavoidably, good and well, but there is no loitering and winding about, as if unwilling to move on till these should suggest themselves . . . and rhetorical embellishments are equally unknown." The truth or falsehood of this statement will, it is hoped, appear in the forthcoming discussion.

The pathos of "The Douglas Tragedy" is, for the moment, a sufficient verification. As is usual in the ballads, the knight and lady, in this particular song, elope, pursued by the damsel's father and seven brothers. The knight kills all, like a doughty lover of old.

> O she's ta'en out her handkerchief,
>   It was o' the holland sae fine,
> And aye she dighted her father's bloody wounds,
>   That were redder than the wine.

> "O chuse, O chuse, Lady Marg'ret," he said,
> "O whether will ye gang or bide?"
> "I'll gang, I'll gang, Lord William," she said,
> "For ye have left me no other guide."
>
> O they rade on and on they rade,
> And a' by the light of the moon,
> Until they came to yon wan water,
> And there they lighted down.
>
> They lighted down to tak a drink
> Of the water that ran so clear;
> And down the stream ran his gude heart's blood,
> And sair she gan to fear.
>
> "Hold up, hold up, Lord William," she says,
> "For I fear that you are slain!"
> "'Tis nothing but the shadow of my scarlet cloak,
> That shines in the water so plain."

And so on. The same quality runs through all.

As might be expected from their origin, the poems are frequently full of metrical anomalies; but of the charm of the style there can be no question. As they are of popular production, we will look in them for no elaborate finish of diction, and no such exalted flights of sentiment as distinguish the verse of schooled poets; but by way of compensation, we will find in these "barbarous productions of unpolished ages," * a strength and vigour that more "polished" performances often lack.

One thing more must be noted in the discussion of the character of these poems. The formulaic or commonplace lines are remarkably numerous throughout the ballad literature, and seem to have been the common property of the bards. Whether used as helps to memory, or as stimulant of pleasure for the auditor, they are uniquely prevalent in the popular song. Readers of Homer know the charm that comes from the recurrence of his formulaic lines, and the more limited body of Anglo-Saxon students will remember the formulaic epithets and lines in the Beowulf and the poems of Cynewulf, a model to which Tennyson may have gone for the beautiful repetitions that accent the loveliness of the "Idylls."

* See Percy, Dedication to first edition of the Reliques.

These repetitions in the ballads are found in the use of stock epithets for certain things. Thus nearly every horse is "milk-white," a quality pertaining, likewise, to every lady's hand that is not "lily" or "lilly" or "lillye," as the case may be. The sword is "berry-brown," and the greenwood is ever "merry."

In addition, whole stanzas are repeated by different poets, with more freedom, even, than Greek commonplaces by the Attic orators. Mr. Motherwell notes the commonplace of the burial of two lovers:

> Lord William was buried in St. Marie's Kirk,
>   Lady Marg'ret in the quire;
> Out of the lady's grave grew a bonny red rose,
>   And out o' the Knight's a brier.
>
> And they twa met, and they twa plat,
>   And fain they wad be near;
> And a' the warld might ken right weel,
>   They were twa lovers dear.

The little boy that runs errands is also invariably described in one way:

> And when he came to the broken brigg,
>   He bent his bow and swam;
> And when he came to the grass growing,
>   Set down his feet and ran, etc.

Another remarkable case is that of the man in haste:

> "Go saddle to me the black,
>   Go saddle to me the brown,
> Go saddle to me the swiftest steed
>   That e'er rade frae the town."

The ballads charm by their simplicity; compared with the artificial poetry of the age of Percy—the remains of the Pope school—they are marvels of poetic spirit, and it is not to be wondered at that in revolt against that artificiality, the Reliques should have been taken up with an eagerness that may strike some to-day as marvellous. They brought back the true song, and have had an effect on our latter-day poetry. The danger seems to be in estimating them above their value; poetic beauties they have of high order, but poetic grace and finish they lack in large degree. A sure insight will enable us to place these ballads in true perspective in English literature, and enjoy them none the less because they are overshadowed by the productions of "clerkly writers," singing for fame as well as for money.

ON FIGURES IN GENERAL IN THE BALLADS.

The ballads, then, being the artless expression of national popular feeling, we will scarcely look in them for the figures that come from deep observation of men and the world. Such figures as occur are generally of the most obvious kind, and are used rather for description than for ornament. They spring naturally and inevitably from the subject, as Motherwell says, and are seldom elaborated beyond the physical limit of a single line. The descriptive epithets *milk-white*, *coal-black*, *grass-green*, etc., occur more frequently than any other figure, though it is doubtless true that those expressions had lost then, as now, all suggestion of comparison by simile, and were probably regarded simply as adjectives of colour. Such as they are they are found with amazing frequency in the ballads, *milk-white* alone being used more than sixty times in the eight volumes of Professor Child's Collection of Ballads. The longer similes and metaphors are equally on the surface. *As blythe as bird on tree, as swift as the wind*, etc., similes to-day in common use, are the most usual of those in the ballads, and no better proof of the popular origin of these poems could be urged, than the very frequency in them of such hackneyed expressions. Of course these are the simplest figures found.

In addition, personification plays an important part, and *the raging sea, fortune's smiles*, and *dame fortune unkind*, are as frequently in evidence in these songs, as in the writings of a penny-a-liner. Metonymy, too, is common. The *merry greenwood*, *dizzy crag*, etc., will be noted in their proper places.

Beyond these more ordinary figures of thought—tropes, to keep the old word—it is not the purpose of this essay to go. The more usual forms of rhetorical figures of style and arrangement—balance, antithesis, chiasmus, etc.—are occasionally met with, more or less perfect in form, but from the very nature of the origin of these songs, it will readily be seen how impossible it was for the finer beauties of style to abound in them or even to be cultivated beyond the merest chance or the most naïve endeavour.

But this is not all, though it must be confessed that it is the greater part. Figures of the foregoing simplicity are, indeed, the rule in the ballads, but occasionally the reader meets with flashes of imagination that surprise him by their brilliancy. These figures generally spring from resemblances to nature. A striking simile in "The Marriage of Sir Gawaine" is

> I am glad as grasse wold be of raine,

and in "Andrew Lammie,"

> Her *bloom* was *like the springing flower*,
> That *salutes* the *rosy* morning.

Again, a strong bit from the "Gay Goshawk" is worth repeating for its unusual length:

> The thing of my love's face that's white
> Is that of dove or maw;
> The thing of my love's face that's red,
> Is like blood shed on snaw.

Figures drawn from the contemplation of man as a moral and intellectual agent are rare. We find the adjectives *princely*, *royal*, etc., but we do not get into the heart of man. Such similes as Coleridge's (in "The Rime of the Ancient Mariner")

> Like one that on a lonesome road
> Doth walk in fear and dread, etc.

are never found in the ballads, and the employment of such a comparison by Coleridge marks his departure from the true ballad style, which he successfully hits in *red as a rose is she*, and in other places. The simile beginning *like one that on a lonesome road*, is singularly beautiful, too beautiful by far for the apprehension or production of a popular poet. It may be good art, but it is not good ballad writing.

Enough has been said to shew the general nature of the ballad figures; they will now be taken up in detail.

We may well close this preliminary discussion by bringing up a parallel from two poems on the same subject—one the ballad from Percy known as "King Arthur's Death," the other, Tennyson's noble "Passing of Arthur." No amount of critical writing could so aptly prove the difference between untrained art and the art that springs from the highest poetical gifts. In citing these instances, however, it must be remembered that "King Arthur's Death" is not one of the best of the ballads, being inferior in every way to such pieces as "Cospatrick," "Gil Morice," or many others that could be mentioned; it must be remembered, also, that Tennyson is not a representative poet, since he is too great, too striking to be compared with any but himself. If, therefore, we bear these facts in mind, we will not be misled by the parallel. The scene is that night-vision of Arthur's before the last great battle with Modred. The ballad is quoted from the Percy Folio MS., without Percy's emendations, and there and in Tennyson, it reads as follows:

KING ARTHUR'S DEATH.

But vpon Sunday in the euening then,
   when the King in his bedd did Lye,
he thought Sir Gawaine to him came,
   & thus to him did say :

"Now as you are my vnkle deere,
   I pray you be ruled by mee,
do not fight as to-morrow day
   but put the battelle of if you may ;

for Sir Lancelott is now in france,
   & many Knights with him full hardye,
& with-in this Month here hee wilbe great aide wilbe to thee."

THE PASSING OF ARTHUR.

Then ere that last weird battle in the west,
There came on Arthur sleeping, Gawain kill'd
In Lancelot's war, the ghost of Gawain blown
Along a wandering wind, and past his ear
Went shrilling : "Hollow, hollow all delight.
Hail, King! To-morrow thou shalt pass away.
Farewell! there is an isle of rest for thee :
And I am blown along a wandering wind,

he wakened forth of his dreemes :
   to his nobles that told hee,
how he thought Sir Gawaine to him
   came,
& these words sayd Certainly.

And hollow, hollow, hollow all delight."
And fainter onward, like wild birds
   that change
Their season in the night and wail
   their way
From cloud to cloud, down the long
   wind the dream
Shrill'd; but in going mingled with
   dim cries
Far in the moonlit haze among the
   hills,
As of some lonely city sack'd by night,
When all is lost, and wife and child
   with wail
Pass to new lords; and Arthur woke
   and call'd
" Who spake? A dream. O light upon
   the wind,
Thine, Gawain, was the voice—are
   these dim cries
Thine? or doth all that haunts the
   waste and wild
Mourn, knowing it will go along with
   me?"

There, in brief, is the difference, as respects figure and every poetical grace, except, at times, "high seriousness," between ballads and the "productions of clerks in closet."

Writing like this of Tennyson's is apt to lift you from your critical feet in a high gale of enthusiasm; the ballad literature at its best leaves the ear sensitive to metrical faults, even while it moves the heart with unexpected feeling.

THE DIVISION OF THE SUBJECT.

For practical purposes the following division of the subject may be made:

Simile and Metaphor—subdivided into three classes:

   A. Figures of Resemblance drawn from the Domain of Nature.
   B. Figures of Resemblance drawn from Animals and their Characteristics.

C. Figures of Resemblance drawn from Man and his Habits.

Metonymy and Personification—briefly considered.

A.

Simile and Metaphor Drawn from the Domain of Nature.

As in the case of all true poets, the main source of inspiration for the balladists is in the κόσμος or ordered creation about them. Man in his various relations to the world and to his destiny is their theme; but man cannot be viewed apart from his environment, especially his physical environment. Hence the repeated allusion, though never so brief, to the scene of the ballad-story; and hence the source of the greater number of the figures that explain, not adorn, the ballad narratives. The old minstrels saw the world, that it was fair; that on happy days the sky was clear, that the sun shed a golden haze, that the grass was green, and that in the spreading trees, birds sang the morning hours away. Little more than this appealed to these crude poets. Doubtless the sun sometimes failed to appear and the grass was sodden with rain, but for all poetical purposes, the minstrels chose as far as possible to ignore the fact. Therefore, though the rain falls, we are for the most part conscious from our ballad-reading, that the sun shines more than half the year. In the Robin Hood stories, for instance, storm seldom comes to the merry greenwood, and the outlaw and his band stand out against a background of perfect weather.

Brilliancy of imagery and wealth of colour, in fact, everywhere abound in the ballads. This brightness is one of the most conspicuous features even of the saddest history. A large number, then, of the similes and metaphors in the popular song is suggested by this aspect of the English landscape, clad in its summer garb of green boughs and green fields under dazzling skies. And yet the figures drawn therefrom admit of division into various groups, according as they arise from one or another aspect of this glad world. It is permissible, therefore, to employ the following arrangement of the figures of resemblance drawn from nature.

    I. Figures drawn from the Physical World of the Wind, Rocks, Water, the Heavens, etc.
    II. Figures drawn from the Plant World.
    III. Figures involving Colour.
    IV. Figures drawn from the Mineral Kingdom.
    V. Figures drawn from the Characteristics of Fire.

These divisions will naturally encroach on one another, and blend together, but care will be taken to keep them as distinct as possible.

I.

Similes and Metaphors from the Physical Aspect of Nature.

Though the bright sun and the fair sky are most prominent in the poems, yet the irresistible forces of nature seem, under this head, to have been a great source of imaginative comparison to the popular poet. Chief among these forces is that of the invisible but mighty w i n d. This is a fruitful theme for the untrained, as for the trained imagination. Let us instance the figures thence derived, to be found throughout the ballads:

In Thomas the Rhymer, 32 (Vol. i, page 110) we find

    The steed flew swifter than the wind;

and again, 34,

    The steed gaed swifter than the wind.

Many similar cases occur elsewhere:

    They passed as swift as any wind.
        —*The Suffolk Miracle*, 50 (i, 220);

    He amblit like the wind.
        —*Lord Thomas and Fair Annet*, 62 (ii, 128);

    The horse zoung Waters rade upon
    Was fleeter than the wind.
        —*Young Waters*, 15–16 (iii, 89);

> As swift as the wind to ride they were seen.
> —*The Blind Beggar's Daughter of Bednall Green*, 93 (iv, 166) ;

> Y schall her sende a wheyt palffrey,
> Het hambellet as the weynde.
> —*Robin Hood and the Potter*, 287-288 (v, 31).

A more extended simile is found in

> "Sweevens are swift, master," quoth John,
> "As the wind that blowes ore a hill ;
> For if it be never so loud this night,
> To-morrow it may be still."
> —*Robin Hood and Guy of Gisborne*, 17-20 (v, 160).

There can be no reasonable doubt that this simile, at least, belongs by right of inheritance to the English ballad. Then, again, the man is compared once, morally, to variable winds or "kittle-flaws" in

> The Gordons they are *kittle-flaws*.
> —*Huntley's Retreat*, 105 (vii, 273).

The wind "hambellet" and is, therefore, a symbol of swiftness or of change and instability, but the s t o n e s and the r o c k s and mountains remain forever the same, teaching their lesson to men. The cruelty of rocks—their unflinching opposition to human strength—is a common inheritance of man, at least in a literary sense. This aspect of nature is fully recorded by the minstrels, and hence they draw one of their most numerous classes of figures.

And first as to the stillness of the rocks, we find :

> Thomas still als stane he stude.
> —*Thomas of Ersseldoune*, 179 (i, 105) ;

> Wel stille I stod als did the stane.
> —*Als I Yod on Ay Mounday*, 33 (i, 274) ;

> He stood as still as rock of stane.
> —*Kinmont Willie*, 178 (vi, 66);

> Some fell in swonyng as thei were dede,
> And lay still as ony stone.
> —*Robin Hood and the Monk*, 121-122 (v, 6).

A new epithet for stone is in the following solitary instance:

> The young men answer'd never a word,
> They were dumb as a stane.
> —*Robin Hood and the Beggar*, 215–216 (v, 202).

And rocks and mountains are h i g h , though scarcely noted as such in the ballads, the two succeeding examples exhausting the subject; perhaps owing to the physical conditions of the Scotch and English birth-place of the ballad:

> To lift him as high as a rock.
> —*The Dragon of Wantley*, 132 (viii, 133);

and

> The swelling seas ran mountain-high.
> —*Fair Margaret of Craignargat*, 103 (viii, 253).

The same idea may be in

> he will to honour climb.
> —*The Seven Champions*, 32 (i, 84);

or is the traditional ladder signified here?

But, after all, the most apparent attribute of rock is i m p e n e t r a b i l i t y , and the comparison of this quality with human cruelty is one of the most obvious thoughts, and has so obtained since the dawn of literature that to-day "a stony heart" is a term perfectly understood, and not easily to be translated into less figurative language. The ballad-writers, of course, are not slow to realise this truth. Some instances are these that follow:

> And hee tooke up the Eldryge sworde,
> As hard as any fflynt.*
> —*Sir Cauline*, 145–146 (iii, 180);

> O spare, if in your bluidy breast,
> Abides not heart of stane.
> —*Lammikin*, 85–86 (iii, 310);

> Her heart's hard as marble.
> —*Willow, Willow, Willow*, 19 (iv, 235);

and

> her hart as hard as stone.
> —*Queen Dido*, 50 (viii, 209).

* Corrected from the Percy MS.

Two similar comparisons are these isolated ones, both implying the irresistible force of rock:

> His strength of stane.
> —*Auld Maitland*, 56 (vi, 222);

and

> Ant al hem to-dryven ase ston doth the glas.
> —*The Flemish Insurrection*, 39 (vi, 270).

Another obvious attribute of stone is c o l d n e s s. Here again, the ballads lead the way. And similarly, in this connection the coldness of clay may be cited.

> And clay-cold were her rosy lips.
> —*The Lass of Lochroyan*, 143 (ii, 112);

> O wan and cold as clay,
> —*Sweet Willie and Fair Annie*, 158 (ii, 139);

and in the same poem, " clay-cold lip " again occurs. And once more:

> Till she fell down at Willie's feet,
> As cauld as ony stone.
> —*Sweet Willie and Fair Maisry*, 127–128 (ii, 337);

and

> He kissed her cold lips, which were colder than stane.
> —*Lord Salton and Auchanarchie*, 55 (ii, 170).

In the famous "Children in the Wood," 53 (iii, 131), we also find

> With lippes as cold as any stone.

Here is the chill of fear in " The Nut-browne Maide," 141–142 (iv, 149).

> it makith myn herte
> As cold as ony ston;

and,

> With a heart more cold than any stone.
> —*The Famous Flower of Servingmen*, 20 (iv, 175).

The harmless stone again takes another aspect in this solitary instance:

> Wha sits into the Troughend Tower,
> Wi' heart as *black* as any stone.
> —*The Death of Parcy Reed*, 57–58 (vi, 146).

Another element of the physical world made to stand in opposition to man and his desires is the overwhelming force of w a t e r c o u r s e s and of the s e a. We have already noted the personification of the sea, by applying to it such epithets as *raging, angry,* etc.; we shall also find occasional similes drawn from the same source in the ballad literature. And indeed, readers of Cynewulf and the early Saxon poets do not need to be reminded of the antiquity of these comparisons in English literature.

Take this from the ballads:

> How can ze strive against the stream?
> For I sall be obeyd.
> —*Gil Morice*, 21–22 (ii, 32);

or this:

> The shallowest water makes maist din,
> The deadest pool the deepest linn;
> The richest man least truth within,
> Though he preferred be.
> —*Fair Helen*, 9–12 (ii, 209);

or,

> Nor rinning ance sae like a sea.
> —*Jack o' the Side*, 112 (vi, 86);

and

> It was flowing like the sea.
> —*Archie of Ca'field*, 92 (vi, 92);

> Now have they taken the wan water,
> Though it was roaring like the sea.
> —*Billie Archie*, 61–62 (vi, 96),

and in the same poem (line 46),

> It now was rumbling like the sea.

And again we have the gentler aspect of f o u n t a i n s, etc., in

> Her eyes like fountains running.
> —*The King of France's Daughter*, 98 (iv, 219),

or in

> While crystal tears, like fountains ran.
> —*Fair Margaret of Craignargat*, 107 (viii, 253),

a style of figure very frequent in the sentimental school of ballads to which the first of these quotations is to be referred. With these it is interesting to compare Percy's own graft on the defenceless "Child of Elle,"

> The tears that fell from her fair eyes,
> Ranne like the fountayne free.
> —*Child of Elle*, 95-96 (iii, 228),

a figure no better and no worse than its models. Finally we may note

> Which made it look just like a brook,
> Running with burning brandy.
> —*The Dragon of Wantley*, 47-48 (viii, 130).

We will not leave the adverse aspects of nature without citing the storms and elemental disturbances, which go so far to afflict man when in direct contact with uncultivated nature. We shall find these aspects of the heavens serving in the ballads as sources of figures, and the similes and metaphors drawn from the phenomena of rain, hail, thunder, frost, and the snow (except colour-similes), are here grouped under one head, in the belief that they are sufficiently alike to warrant such treatment.

The comparisons from the r a i n are as numerous as any in this group, and yet not frequent. They are as simple as follows:

> Till the bloode from the bassonetts ranne,
> As the roke * doth in the rayne.
> —*The Battle of Otterbourne*, 89-90 (vii, 15);

> And the blood ran down like rain.
> —*Battle of Otterbourne*, B, 84 (vii, 23);

> Till the bloode owte off thear basnets sprente,
> As ever dyd heal or rayne.
> —*The Hunting of the Cheviot*, 31 (vii, 36);

and again,

> But yt was marvele and the red blude ronne not,
> As the reane doys in the stret.
> —*The Hunting of the Cheviot*, 175-176 (vii, 42);

---

* Roke—reek or smoke.

and finally,

> Until the blood, like drops of rain.
> —*Chevy Chace*, 127 (vii, 4º).

It will be noted that these similes are all alike. A curious fact is that they are found only in two poems of great similarity. The reader can draw his own conclusion. Once again:

> As e'er you saw the rain down fa',
> Or yet the arrow frae the bow,
> Sae our Scottish lads fell even down.
> —*The Battle of Loudon Hill*, 41–43 (vii, 151);

and

> Quhair bulletis, dartis, and arrowes flew,
> Als thick as haill or raine.
> —*The Battle of Balrinnes*, 229–230 (vii, 226).

A different point of view is that of the following:

> And brothers Balfours they stood the first *show'rs* [of arrows].
> —*The Battle of Sheriff-Muir*, 59 (vii, 160);

and in this:

> Led Camerons on in *clouds*, man.
> —*The Battle of Tranent-Muir*, 10 (vii, 168);

and again,

> And the *clouds* of arrows flew.
> —*Robin Hood and the Valiant Knight*, 229–230 (v, 391).

We have at least one good simile drawn from the sting of the h a i l:

> The blows fell thick as bickering hail.
> —*Jamie Telfer*, 134 (vi, 112).

The t h u n d e r fares better and receives due consideration in these four figures:

> For a cannon's roar, in a summer's night,
> Is like thunder in the air.
> —*Bonny John Seton*, 59–60 (vii, 234).

And similarly,

> For their cannons roar like thunder.
> —*Undaunted Londonderry*, 5 (vii, 249);

and
>
> Thundering stones they laid on the walls.
> —*Ibid.*, 25 (vii, 249).

Once more,
> Golden (!) fame did thunder.
> —*The King of France's Daughter*, 176 (iv, 223).

The f r o s t is recognised twice, independently.
> Sen ze by me will nae be warned
> In it ze sall find frost.
> —*Gil Morice*, 41–42 (ii, 32);

which reminds one of Persius' "chilling threshold,"
> Vide sis, ne maiorum tibi forte
> limina frigescant.
> —Sat. I, 108–109.

And in this good moral reflection:
> Fals waes here foreward so forst is in May,
> That sonne from the southward wypeth away.
> —*The Execution of Sir Simon Fraser*, 42–43 (vi, 276).

The s n o w, except for the expression "snow-white," which will be treated under colour-similes, is sparingly drawn on for figurative illustration. Joined with the frost it is found in the following concealed simile:
> 'T is not the frost that freezes fell,
> Nor blawing snaw's inclemency;
> 'T is not sic cauld that makes me cry,
> But my love's heart grown cauld to me.
> —*Waly Waly, but Love be Bonny*, 25–28 (iv, 134).

The n i g h t is used once as a simile for darkness:
> Whare it was dirk as mydnyght myrke.
> —*Thomas of Ersseldoune*, 117 (i, 103).

In other poems coal and pitch and tar are the similes for darkness; terms which will be treated in their proper places under colour-similes.

We have purposely exhausted the gloomy side of nature before turning to the brighter world of sun and passing shower. Here we find the beauty and freshness of the spring where, though the rain may fall, it is turned into jewel-drops by the peeping sun. These figures are less varied in the ballads, and may be dismissed with fewer words than those which preceded.

To take up the s u n similes first, we find

> Als dose the sonne on someres daye,
> That faire lady hir selfe scho schone.
> —*Thomas of Ersseldoune*, 20 (i, 98).

And again,

> How art thu fadyde thus in the face
> That schane byfore als the sonne so bryght?
> —*Ibid.*, 101-102 (i, 102).

In another poem,

> She cast an eye on little Musgrave,
> As bright as the summer sun.
> —*Little Musgrave and the Lady Bernard*, 13-14 (ii, 16);

and once more,

> And when she cam into the kirk,
> She shimmer'd like the sun.
> —*Lord Thomas and Fair Annet*, 77-78 (ii, 128).

The m o o n is noticed twice, once favourably, and once unfavourably:

> this worldis blisse
> That chaungeth as the mone.
> —*The Nutbrowne Maide*, 61-62 (iv, 146).

This beautiful solitary instance occurs in Lord John, 20 (i, 135):

> Gaed as licht as a glint o' the moon.

Once we find

> She is neither white nor brown,
> But as the heavens fair.
> —*As I Came from Walsingham*, 9-10 (iv, 192).

The morning d e w and the passing s h o w e r next claim our attention. Twice, and in different versions of the same ballad occurs the line

> And fades away like the morning dew.
> { —*Waly, Waly, but Love be Bonny*, 12 (iv, 133).
> { —*Lord Jamie Douglas*, 8 (iv. 136);

and again we find the beautiful simile

> They ley likes na the summer shower,
> Nor girse the mornin dew,
> Better, dear Lady Maisry,
> Than Chil Ether loves you.
> —*Chil Ether*, 5–8 (iv, 299),

and once more in a later ballad,

> And from her cleare and cristall eyes
> The tears gusht out apace,
> Which, like the silver-pearled deaw, etc.
> —*Fair Rosamond*, 69–71 (vii, 286).

The changeableness of summer days, finally, is witnessed by this from "The Nutbrowne Maide," 61–64 (iv, 146):

> O Lorde, what is this worldis blisse
> That chaungeth as the mone;
> My somers day in lusty May
> Is derked before the none;

and in this striking phrase,

> Hii maden kyng of somer.
> —*Execution of Sir Simon Fraser*, 66 (vi, 277).

Summary.—The figures, then, in this subdivision of the subject, are frequent exactly in proportion to the obviousness of the relationship expressed; and the figures most common in the ballads are those heard oftenest in colloquial speech. "Swift as the wind," "cold" or "hard" as stone, "bright as the sun," "loud as thunder" (at least by implication) are most in ballad use, and just so far as a ballad abounds in these simple similes may we with more authority vouch for its genuineness.

II.

Similes and Metaphors drawn from Plant Life.

Here the same remarks are applicable that were in force in the preceding section. There is nothing elaborate, nothing but what is before the eyes. The bird on the tree, the rustling foliage, the springing flower, are much in evidence, and the commonest metaphor is the bestowing of the term "flower" on persons of either sex, distinguished for beauty or virtue. We shall take up the figures in detail, in order of their logical development.

The object most apparent in the first view of the world of growth is the grass at our feet, seen everywhere and become a part of our thought. The simile "grass-green," then, is natural, and in the ballads it is frequent. Later we shall see how strong was the love of colour in these poems and how reasonable it is to find in them "grass-green" and "milk-white," used together for purposes of contrast. Formulaic as any are these lines,

> He took her by the milk-white hand,
> And by the grass-green sleeve;

but this belongs more properly to the chapter on colour-similes and to that we leave it.

Once occurs the striking simile

> I am glad as grasse wold be of raine.
> —*The Marriage of Sir Gawaine*, 200 (i, 38),

in a ballad of the Percy folio, and therefore authentic.

But it is ever the exception that attracts most attention. We see many sunny days, but it is the lowering heaven that lifts our eyes—mostly in doubt—to the sky. The grass, too, is much commoner that the flower, yet it is the flower that receives most frequent mention in popular literature. These flower-similes are, in fact, the most plentiful crop that the balladist gathers on his imaginative journey through the world. It would be impossible to quote all the instances, and we must, therefore, content ourselves with citing the most remarkable.

The metaphor by which a person of striking qualities, physical or moral, is called a flower is perpetuated to-day in colloquial English as it was in colloquial Greek, and undoubtedly in the popular speech of all nations. Instances in the ballads are the following:

> I dreamt that Annie of Lochroyan,
> The flower o' a' her kin.
> —*Annie of Lochroyan*, 97-98 (ii, 103).

> The fairest flower's cut down by love,
> That e'er sprung up in Fyvie.
> —*Andrew Lammie*, 187-188 (ii, 199).

> The flower of my affected heart,
> Whose sweetness doth excell.
> —*Fair Rosamond*, 53-54 (vii, 286).

> Of all fairheid scho bur the flour.
> *The Bloody Sark*, 9 (viii, 148).

More striking is the expression

> Untimely crop some virgin flowr.
> —*St. George and the Dragon*, 50 (i, 74).

That courtesy was not everywhere in evidence in these poems of the age of chivalry is shown by the line,

> O hold your tongue, my sprightly flower.
> —*James Herries*, 61 (i, 207).

The particular kind of flower is sometimes specified; occasionally it is a rose, more frequently a lily. Note the following:

> Come ben,* come ben, my lily flower.
> —*Young Akin*, 207 (i, 188),

and,

> Gang to your bouirs, ye lilye flouirs.
> —*The Clerk's Twa Sons o' Owsenford*, 77 (ii, 67).

A formulaic line, this last, met sometimes in the singular:

> Gang to your bower, my lily flower.
> —*Blancheflour and Jellyflorice*, 81 (iv, 298).

A more original bit is this:

> A fairer rose did never bloom
> Than now lies cropped on Yarrow.
> —*The Dowie Dens of Yarrow*, 67-68 (iii, 68).

Once more,

> The fairest rose in all the world.
> —*Fair Rosamond*, 51 (vii, 286).

* Ben—quickly.

Compare in Shakspere, Laertes' impassioned

> O rose of May!
> Dear maid, kind sister, sweet Ophelia.
> —*Hamlet*, iv, 5, 140,

and the well-known

> Elaine, the lily maid of Astolat.

Mixed metaphor is rare; the following, however, is certainly susceptible to that charge:

> For the fair *flower* of England will never *shine* more.
> —*Queen Jeanie*, 36 (vii, 76).

The radical metaphor in the verb *flourish* occurs, and is submitted here with the reservation that, as the balladists probably knew nothing of the figure in question, they used it simply, without premeditation. The instances are these:

> The London dames, in Spanish pride,
> Did *flourish* everywhere.
> —*Queen Eleanor's Fall*, 21-22 (vii, 293).

> There he *flourisht* many a day.
> —*Thomas Stukeley*, 58 (vii, 309).

Or,

> Who on the throne does flourish and reign.
> —*Undaunted Londonderry*, 62 (vii, 250).

Another verbal metaphor is the solitary use of *flower* as a verb in the threat to the offender,

> Thou shalt be the first man
> Shall *flower* this gallows tree.
> —*Robin Hood and the Old Man*, 64-65 (v, 260).

Once more, there is a metaphor concealed in the term "the *drooping* king." ("The Seven Champions," 102, i, 87.)

Passing from metaphor to simile, we find the lily and the rose contending for mastership as in one of the similes to be adduced in another connexion; and sometimes again, the species of flower is left to the imagination. Instance the following:

> Her bloom was like the springing flower
> That salutes the rosy morning.
> —*Andrew Lammie*, 5-6 (ii, 191).

> For the flower that springs in May morning,
> Was not sae sweet as she.
> —*The Gay Goss-Hawk*, 47-48 (iii, 279).

> She brightened like the lily-flower.
> —*Ibid.*, 137 (iii, 283).

Or,

> Earl Richard had but ae daughter,
> Fair as a lily-flower.
> —*Birth of Robin Hood*, 5-6 (v, 170).

Again,

> Till she wallow't * like a lily.
> —*Geordie* (A), 12 (viii, 93).

To which we may compare,

> She's wallowed like a weed.
> —*The Jolly Goshawk*, 114 (iii, 290).

Finally, we may cite,

> But like the rose among the throng
> Was the lady and her maries fair.
> —*The Hireman Chiel*, 214-215 (viii, 241).

The sweetness of flowers, too, is probably the source of the expression, "my sweet love," etc. This is proved by the verse already quoted,

> The flower of my affected heart,
> Whose *sweetness* doth excell;

again, we have,

> To hang the *flower* o' Scottish land,
> Sae *sweet* and fair a boy.
> —*Gilderoy*, 85-86 (vi, 201),

and

> My *sweet*, bonnie Lady.
> —*Geordie* (A), 60 (viii, 95).

More materially,

> A breath as sweet as rose.
> —*Gilderoy*, 10 (vi, 198).

After flowers, the t r e e s. To the popular poet, the joyousness and lightness of the summer foliage was the salient feature of tree life. This is evidenced by the following large group:

> Robene on his wayis went,
> As licht as leif of tre.
> —*Robene and Makyne*, 65-66 (iv, 248).

---

* Withered.

> And Robyn was in mery Scherwode
> As lizt as lef on lynde.
> —*Robin Hood and the Monk*, 300–301 (v, 14).

> Thus be these good yemen gone to the wood
> As lyght as lefe on lynde.
> —*Adam Bel, Clym of the Cloughe*, etc., 171–172 (v, 145).

And once, the following,

> She's as jimp in the middle,
> As ony willow-wand.
> —*The Laird of Waristoun*, 7–8 (iii, 107).

This idea of the lightness of leaves is given a distinctly humorous turn in the clever ballad of the "Wanton Wife of Bath," 77–78 (viii, 155) where

> "They say," quoth Thomas, "women's tongues
> Of aspen leaves are made."

The birds and their song are so important a part of the visible landscape that it is with difficulty we refrain from introducing the bird-similes in this place; but on reflection it seems perhaps better to relegate these figures, "blythe as bird on tree," etc., to the second great division of the subject—Figures drawn from Animals and their Characteristics.

The s t r e n g t h of trees tempts the popular bard to a comparison with stiffness of moral purpose.

> I leaned my back unto an aik,
> I thought it was a trusty tree;
> But first it bow'd, and syne it brak,
> Sae my true love did lightly me!
> —*Waly, Waly, but Love be Bonny*, 5–8 (iv, 133).

Again:

> But yet we will not slander them all,
> For there is of them good enow;
> It is a sore consumed tree,
> That on it bears not one fresh bough.
> —*Rookhope Ryde*, 9–12 (vi, 122).

Once more,

> Thir Weardale men, they have good hearts,
> They are as stiff as any tree.
> —*Ibid.*, 137–138 (vi, 129).

Similar enough to be quoted is this:

> There's nane may lean on a rotten staff,
> But him that risks to get a fa';
> There's nane may in a traitor trust,
> And traitors black were every Ha'.
> —*The Death of Parcy Reed*, 49–52 (vi, 142).

A use of **hedge** for strength or defence is familiar to students of Anglo-Saxon literature and of Beowulf in particular. In the ballads we find

> He was a hedge unto his friends,
> A heckle* to his foes, lady.
> —*Rob Roy*, 53–54 (vi, 200).

The **greenness** and **pith**—in other words, the strength and vigour of plant-life are instanced here:

(1) Thy thoughts are greene.
—*Gentle Herdsman, Tell to Me*, 14 (iv, 188),

(2) —and Glangary's pith, too.
—*The Battle of Sheriff-Muir*, 31 (vii, 159);

and their opposites in the following:

(1) Love liketh not the fallen fruit,
Nor the withered tree.
—*As I Came from Walsingham*, 27–28 (iv, 192).

(2) The beggar answered *cankerdly*.
—*Robin Hood and the Beggar*, 51 (v, 190).

(3) But with *crosse-grain'd* words they did him thwart.
—*Robin Hood's Progress*, Introd. 3 (v, 290).

The **fruit** of the tree is seldom noted. We find once

> Ilka ee intil her head
> Was like a rotten ploom.
> —*Kempy-Kaye*, 41–42 (viii, 141);

but this, like the *kaily lips*, (*cabbage-like* lips) of the same poem, is a special comparison applied to a particular case, and deserves no notice, not having a bearing on figures in general—those that occur with comparative frequency throughout the ballads.

---

* Heckle—hatchel, flax-comb.

"Smells not like balsam"* is another solitary instance, proving nothing. Once, too, we find

> I was once as fow of Gill Morice,
> As the hip † is o' the stean.
> —*Gil Morice*, 143-144 (ii, 371).
>
> She burned like hollin-green.
> —*Earl Richard* 120 (iii, 9),

is a comparison found once, and good to that extent. And "as fair's a cypress queen" (John o' Hazelgreen, 120, iv, 88) used also but once, will end the list of sporadic illustrations drawn from plant life.

Summary.—Figures of resemblance, then, in the plant world, drawn from the green grass, the flowers, particularly the rose and the lily, from the foliage and strength of trees, are common enough; those drawn from such sources, accordingly, would be good evidence, other things being equal, of the popular origin of a ballad. Rarer use is made of the hedge (familiar, as we saw, in Anglo-Saxon), the canker of trees, etc., and the ballad that employs figures drawn therefrom, is on that account less liable to complete acceptance. It is, as will have been observed, in this province of the natural world, that some of the greatest numbers of repetitions of simile and metaphor occur; the result is put forward without further comment, as only one conclusion may be reached from it.

III.

Similes and Metaphors of Colour.

Colour is the one thing everywhere prominent in the ballads. Everything sparkles; the lawn is green, the sky is fair; the lady's hand is milk-white, her dress is green as grass; her cheek is rosy, her lip cherry and sometimes ruby; her hair is like the "mowten" gold. Every colour has its characteristic epithet, and the epithet is employed again and again.

As we began, in describing the similes drawn from nature,

---

* The Dragon of Wantley, 110 (viii, 132).
† Hip = berry.

with the darker or adverse phenomena, so in colour-similes we will begin with the expressions denoting white and black, the absence, if you please, of all colour. And first, the natural similes implying w h i t e n e s s demand our attention. It has already been said that the epithet "milk-white" occurs more than sixty times in the ballads; indeed, as the diminutives in -*let* have been burlesqued by modern bards, so the stately "milk-white" has lost for more sophisticated readers its former aptness, in the play of humour that to-day is sure to put it in solution. In the ballads the simile is used to describe various things. In Thomas the Rhymer, 29 (i, 110),

> She mounted on her milk-white steed ;

and in young Tamlane, 149 (i, 121),

> For I will ride on the milk-white steed.

Again,

> O where were ye, my milk-white steed ?
> —*The Broomfield Hill*, 33 (i, 133).

Many instances of "milk-white" steed occur throughout these songs.

The expression is applied likewise to hands:

> She took me up in her milk-white hands.
> —*Alison Gross*, 49 (i, 170).

And in the formulaic line:

> He's taen her by the milk-white hand,

which occurs among other places in Tam-a-Line, 25 (i, 259). Again

> O laith, laith were our guid lords' sons
> To weet their milk-white hands.
> —*Sir Patrick Spens*, 94 (iii, 341).

But other things are also milk-white. In Clerk Tamas 58, (iii, 351),

> Sae did she till her milk-white chin.

In Young Beichan and Susie Pye, 73 (iv, 13):

> Ye set your *milk-white* foot on board.

In King Lear and his Three Daughters, 137 (vii, 281):

> Which made him rend his milk-white locks.

As to the dress of man:

> And he wore a milk-white weed, O.
> —*Sweet Willie and Lady Margerie*, 2 (ii, 53);

and in a variation of the same poem:

> And milk-white was his weed.
> —*Willie and Lady Maisry*, 12 (ii, 57).

The epithet is also applied to other living creatures. A few are the following:

> Your bower was full o' milk-white swans.
> —*Lord Livingston*, 81 (iii, 346).

> There's either a mer-maid or a milk-white swan.
> —*The Cruel Sister*, 63 (ii, 235).

> Then up and crew the milk-white cock.
> —*Clerk Saunders*, 65 (ii, 52).

> And four and twenty milk-white dows.
> —*Lord Wa' Yates and Old Ingram*, 91 (ii, 329).

Again,

> Till by it came, the milk-white hynde.
> —*Leesome Brand*, 67 (ii, 344)

and,

> I have four and twenty milk-white cows
> —*Earl Richard* B, 29 (iii, 267).

The comparison of white objects to milk is also found often in the more direct simile form, "white as milk," or "whiter than milk."

> Your body's whiter than milk.
> —*Clerk Colvill*, 20 (i, 193).

> On his bodye as white as milke.
> —*Child Waters*, 160 (iii, 212).

> And on the block he laid his neck,
> Was whiter than the milk.
> —*Young Waters*, 147-148 (iii, 306).

> Thy pumps as white as was the milk.
> —*Greensleeves*, 31 (iv, 242).

Once, too, we have the same idea in

> She's ty'd it round his whey-white face.
> —*Clerk Colvill*, 28 (i, 193).

But other things beside milk are white. Milk-white, it will be observed, has passed, in modern usage, into snow-white. This comparison is not so common in the ballads, yet it occurs several times. In The Daemon Lover, 71 (i, 204), we find

> O waesome wail'd the snaw-white sprites.

Other examples are these:

> O I will hae the snaw-white boy.
> —*The Cruel Brother*, 25 (ii, 264).

> When the raven shall be white as snow.
> —*The Youth of Rosengord*, 43 (ii, 348).

> He lifted up the snaw-white sheets.
> —*Sir Hugh le Blond*, 51 (iii, 256).

> ann I were as white
> As e'er the snaw lay on the dyke.
> —*The Gaberlunzie Man*, 21-22 (viii, 99).

> The Dinlay snaw was ne'er mair white,
> Nor the lyart* looks of Harden's hair.
> —*Jamie Telfer*, 143-144 (vi, 112).

> Hair black as sloe, skin white as snow.
> —*The Dragon of Wantley*, 69 (viii, 131).

Similarly,

> With her feet as white as sleet.
> —*Sweet Willie and Lady Margerie*, 29 (ii. 54).

The comparison with lilies is, perhaps, even more frequent than the comparison with snow.

> She stretched out her lily-white hand.
> —*Sweet William's Ghost*, 37 (ii. 147).

With which compare Percy's interpolated line:

> Then she held forthe her liley-white hand.
> —*Sir Cauline*, 173 (iii, 181).

"Lily-white hand," indeed, almost divides the honours in the ballads with "milk-white hand."

* Lyart—hoary.

In the following the simile is more concealed:

> O hold your tongue, my lily leesome thing.
> —*James Herries*, 73 (i, 208).

> She's ta'en her by the lily hand.
> —*The Cruel Sister*, 21 (ii, 233).

> Then he cut off her head
> Fra' her lily breast bane.
> —*Lambert Linkin*, 87–88 (iii, 105).

The s w a n also serves, in the popular songs, as a simile for whiteness.

> His heved was wyte als ony swan.
> —*Als I Yod on Ay Mounday*, 21 (i, 274).

> There's twa smocks in your coffer,
> As white as a swan.
> —*Lambert Linkin*, 61–62 (iii, 104).

Similarly, in the two versions of The Gay Goshawk, we find:

> The white that is on her breast bare,
> Like the down o' the white sea-maw.
> —*The Gay Goshawk*, 27–28 (iii, 279),

and

> The thing of my love's face that's white
> Is that of dove or maw.
> —*The Jolly Goss-Hawk*, 9–10 (iii, 285),

a simile whose genuineness is vouched for by existing in two versions.

Once occurs

> O white, white war his wounds washen,
> As white as a linen clout.
> —*Young Redin*, 85–86 (iii, 17),

and once only,

> His beard was all on a white, a,
> As white as whale's bone.
> —*By Landsdale Hey Ho*, 33–34 (v, 432).

With this latter compare Shakspere's

> His teeth as white as whale's bone.
> —*Love's Labours Lost*, v, 2.

Three similes for p a l e n e s s are these :

> And straight againe as pale as lead.
> —*King Kophetua and the Beggar Maid*, 78 (iv, 198) ;

> Sometimes her cheek is rosy red
> And sometimes *deadly* wan.
> —*Burd Ellen*, 89–90 (iii, 217) ;

> More pale she was, when she sought my grace,
> Than prymrose pale and wan.
> —*Jellon Grame*, 73–74 (ii, 289).

The similes of b l a c k n e s s and d a r k n e s s are less common, perhaps from the desire, previously mentioned, on the part of these poets, to represent the bright side of nature in their similes. "Coal-black" is the most frequently used, as in colloquial speech to-day.

> He mounted on his coal-black steed.
> —*Willie and May Margaret*, 5 and 61 (ii, 172 and 174).

> He's set his twa sons on coal-black steeds.
> —*Jamie Telfer*, 81 (vi, 109).

> O laith, laith were our Scots lords' sons
> To weet their coal-black shoon.
> —*Sir Patrick Spens*, 97–98 (iii, 341).

"B l a c k a s a c r o w" (opposed to "white as a swan"), black as pitch or tar, or sable, or night, are common expressions to-day. They occur but rarely in the ballads.

> When the swan is black as night.
> —*The Youth of Rosengood*, 38 (ii, 348).

> With consciences black as a craw, man.
> —*The Battle of Sheriff-Muir*, 46 (vii, 161).

> Wi' their horses black as ony craw.
> —*The Battle of Pentland Hills*, 2 (vii, 241).

Note how these war ballads repeat the same figures, which are found nowhere else. With this compare the blood which "ran like rain" in division I, found only in the battle songs.

Once, again, occur the following:

(1) Though dark the night as pick and tar.
—*Hobie Noble*, 45 (vi, 100).

(2) The night is mirk, and it's very *pit* * mirk.
—*Archie of Ca'field*, 39 (vi, 90).

Only once, too:

Her riding suit was of sable hew black.
—*Robin Hood and the Stranger*, 37 (v, 411).

Likewise, once occurs the well-known simile,

Hair black as sloe.
—*The Dragon of Wantley*, 69 (viii, 131);

and this peculiar one

Ann ye were as black
As e'er the crown of my dady's hat.
—*The Gaberlunzie Man*, 17-18 (viii, 99).

A different figure is the following, yet cited here for completeness:

Yes, I will gae zour *black* errand.
—*Gil Morice*, 39 (ii, 32).

After the white and black, g r e e n and r e d attract our attention. Green, in the expression "grass-green," is very common in the ballads; it does not occur with any object of comparison except grass.

Her shirt was o' the grass-green silk.
—*Thomas the Rhymer*, 5 (i, 109).

And by the grass-green sleeve.
—*Tam-a-Line*, 26 (i, 259).

For thou hast sent her a mantle of greene,
As greene as any grasse.
—*Child Maurice*, 51-52 (ii, 315).

Thy gown was of the grassie green.
—*Greensleeves*, 33 (iv, 242).

And thrice she blew on a grass-green horn.
—*Alison Gross*, 30 (i, 169).

And once, peculiarly,

And out there came the fair Janet,
As green as any grass.
—*The Young Tamlane*, 59-60 (i, 117).

* Pit-mirk—dark as a pit or as pitch? Probably, for phonetic reasons, the former.

Redness is compared indifferently to the rose, the cherry, the ruby, and to blood. As for the rose, we find:

> And clay-cold were her rosy lips.
> —*The Lass of Lockroyan*, 143 (ii, 112).

> The lady blush'd a rosy red.
> —*The Cruel Brother*, 21 (ii, 252).

> And redder than rose her ruddy heart's blood.
> —*Jellon Grame*, 75 (ii, 289).

> He's put it to his red rosy lips.
> —*Earl Robert*, 15 (iii, 27).

> Sometimes her cheek is rosy red.
> —*Burd Ellen*, 90 (iii, 217).

> And drap it on her rose-red lips.
> —*The Gay Goshawk*, 71 (iii, 288).

> And red and rosy was the blood,
> Ran down the lily braes.
> —*Katharine Janfarie*, 67–68 (iv, 32).

And, somewhat differently, we find "rosy morning," Andrew Lammie, 6 (ii, 191).

Another figure is the following:

> The blood within her cristall cheeks
> Did such a cullour drive,
> As though the lilly and the rose
> For mastership did strive.
> —*Fair Rosamond*, 13–16 (vii, 284).

The last, however, is from a ballad of the worst period, when little spontaneity distinguished the productions in this line. Here, for instance, from a ballad standpoint we could wish for more matter with less art. Compare, however, Shakspere's description of Lucrece's beauty:

> This silent war of lilies and of roses
> Which Tarquin viewed in her fair face's field.

A mixture of personification tinges the last comparison under this head,

> And brings a blushing rose.
> —*The Seven Champions*, 110 (i, 88).

As for the cherry comparisons, they all refer to the colouring of the human face:

> O first he kist her cherry cheek.
> —*Fair Annie of Lochroyan*, 129 (ii, 104).
>
> O cherry, cherry was her cheek.
> —*The Lass of Lockroyan*, 141 (ii, 112).
>
> She hath lost her cherry-red.
> —*Fair Margaret and Sweet William*, 48 (ii, 143).
>
> He's put it to his cherry lip.
> —*Prince Robert*, 19 (iii, 23).
>
> And chirry were her cheiks.
> —*Edom o' Gordon*, 74 (vi, 157).

The ruby comparison is interchangeable with rose and cherry similes, but is not so common.

> And sair he kist her ruby lips.
> —*Fair Annie of Lochroyan*, 131 (ii, 104).
>
> With rosy cheek and ruby lip.
> —*The Gay Goshawk*, 139 (iii, 283).

Once only occurs the epithet "coral-red," in a poem, however, whose origin is not popular in the strict sense of the word.

> Her lippes like to a corrall red.
> —*Fair Rosamond*, 73 (vii, 287).

From these examples it will be seen that the descriptions of heroines in modern fiction of a certain rank are builded better than perhaps their authors knew—directly by descent on the firm foundation of popular tradition.

The epithet blood-red is limited to wine, in the ballad literature.

We find in the first lines of Sir Patrick Spence (iii, 149):

> The king sits in Dumferling town,
> Drinking the blude-reid wine.

Again,

> And eneugh of the blood-red wine.
> —*Johnie of Breadislee*, 10 (vi, 12).

Conversely, in The Douglas Tragedy,

> And aye she dighted her father's bloody wounds,
> That were redder than the wine.

And in The Gay Goshawk (the two versions) the redness of blood is used as a simile as follows:

> The red that's on my true love's cheek
> Is like blood-drops in the snaw.
> —*The Gay Goshawk*, 25-26 (iii, 278),

and again,

> The thing of my love's face that's red
> Is like blood shed on snaw.
> —*The Jolly Gos-Hawk*, 11-12 (iii, 285),

which is striking and picturesque, if not a very pretty idea. To conclude, Robin Hood and the Stranger, 14 (v, 405) has the expression,

> His stockings like scarlet shone.

The next colour to receive marked attention is the modest brown. The adjectives n u t-b r o w n and b e r r y-b r o w n must be familiar to all.

> It's ye do kill your berry-brown steed.
> —*King Henry*, 29 (i, 148).

> He's luppen on his berry-brown steed.
> —*The Water o' Wearie's Well*, 9 (i, 199).

> And now he drew his berry-brown sword.
> —*The Laidly Worm of Spindleston-Heugh*, 101 (i, 285),

as peculiar an epithet to apply to a sword, as *nut-brown*, which follows.

The epithet nut-brown is well known from the famous Nutbrowne Maide. A few ballad instances may be cited:

> O sall I tak the nut-browne bride?
> —*Lord Thomas and Fair Annet*, 15 (ii, 126).

Nut-browne is used eight times in this one poem.

> Young Johnstone had a nut-brown sword.
> —*Young Johnston*, 13 (ii, 292).

> And Robin had a nut-brown sword.
> —*Robin Hood and the Beggar*, 46 (v, 253).

A solitary instance:

> But fair fa' that bonnie apple-gray.
> —*Lady Marjorie*, 57 (ii, 340).

The yellow gold and the white silver are everywhere recognised in the ballads, and it is perhaps as well to close the discussion of colour-similes with those drawn from these sources. This plan has been suggested by the fact that it is ever the brilliancy and external showing of these minerals that received most attention from the balladists, and on that account the similes derived therefrom exact classification under the present rather than under the following division of the subject. With this word of explanation, we may proceed to the discussion of the gold and silver similes.

The greater number of the figures suggested by resemblances to gold are used of the hair of individuals.

> The very hair o' my love's head
> Was like the threads o' gold.
> —*James Herries*, 99–100 (i, 209).

> And gowden was her hair.
> —*The Lass of Lochroyan*, 142 (ii, 112).

> The hair that hung owre Johnie's neck shined
> Like the links o' yellow gold.
> —*Johnie Scot*, 75–76 (iv, 54).

> His hair was like the threads o' gowd.
> —*Lord Thomas of Winesberry*, etc., 45 (iv, 307).

> How gowden yellow is your hair.
> —*Lady Elspat*, 2 (iv, 308).

> Her crispéd locks like threedes of gold.
> —*Fair Rosamond*, 9 (vii, 284).

And yet we find it in other connexions. "Glistering like gold" occurs (The Boy and the Mantle, 128, i, 13), and

> And als clere golde her brydill it schone.
> —*Thomas of Ersseldoune*, 85 (i, 99).

> The masts that were like the beaten gold.
> —*The Daemon Lover*, 45 (i, 203).

> And after him a finikin lass
> Did shine like the glistering gold.
> —*Robin Hood and Allin a Dale*, 71–72 (v, 281).

> Whose person was better than gold.
> —*Robin Hood and Maid Marian*, 36 (v, 373).

Gold and silver are combined in the following instances:

> And the topmast and the mainmast,
> Shone like the silver free.
> —*Fair Annie*, 37-38 (iii, 193);

and in the same poem (ll. 41-42),

> And the topmast and the mainmast
> They shone just like the gold.

In Lord Livingston, 23, 25 (iii, 344), we find

> The kipples* were like the gude red gowd,
> And the roof-tree like the siller white.

Summary.—Milk-white, snow-white, lily-white, white as a swan (perhaps), grass-green, rosy, ruby, cherry, berry-brown, nut-brown, golden, glistering like gold, etc., are figures of colour that may pass unquestioned in the ballads; no figures are used oftener and none are more genuine. Other similes from colour there are none, purple, orange, and violet not being represented, and the use of the few mentioned, over and over again, shows how averse the popular poetry must have been to receiving anything novel or sensational in descriptive epithet. The sameness may have palled at times, but it certainly had the effect that old friends have, and on this ground was given a hearty welcome.

IV.

Similes and Metaphors drawn from The Mineral Kingdom.

It has been remarked before, and we shall probably have occasion to remark again, that no division of our subject can be exhaustive. The subdivisions will be found to overlap, and no nice discrimination will entirely satisfy the mind as to which section particular figures should be assigned to. There is no reason, for example, why the figures drawn from gold and silver should not be included in the present instead of the last chapter, and indeed their position at the head of the mineral world seemed to exact such an allotment; the idea of colour is, however, so strong in these similes, that no treatment but

---

* Kipples—rafters.

the one followed seemed either desirable or possible. Strong though the temptation may be to place these figures under any other division of the subject, it is hoped that in the main the distribution here used will not be found unsatisfactory.

The subdivisions in this chapter, which is itself a subdivision, if we exclude the bulk of gold and silver similes, are twofold:

(α). Figures from Crystal and Precious Stones (except the ruby);

(β). Miscellaneous, including a few figures from gold.

(α). Figures drawn from c r y s t a l are not rare. We will quote a few:

> Witness, ye groves and chrystal streams.
> —*The Damosel's Complaint*, 77 (ii, 387).
>
> The crystal tears ran down her face.
> —*The Cruel Black*, 81 (iii, 373).
>
> With chrystal water all in her bright eyes.
> —*The Blind Beggar's Daughter of Bednall Green*, 66 (iv, 171).
>
> His eyes like crystal clear.
> —*Lord Thomas of Winesberry*, 46 (iv, 307).
>
> His eyes they were as cleare
> As christall stone, hey ho.
> —*By Landsdale Hey Ho*, 35–36 (v, 432).
>
> The blood within her cristall cheeks.
> —*Fair Rosamond*, 13 (vii, 284).

"Cristall" as an epithet for cheeks, seems hardly good. In the same poem occurs the *silver-pearled* dew, adversely noted, and which is found nowhere else. It does not lighten the general doubt as to the worth of this ballad.

> And from her cleare and cristall eyes
> The tears gusht out apace,
> Which, like the silver-pearled deaw, etc.
> —*Fair Rosamond*, 69-71 (vii, 286).

It will be seen that all, or nearly all, of these examples are taken from the ballads of a certain period, when ballad-writing was descending into ballad-mongering. The authors of Gil Morice and Fair Annet had no time to waste on such puerilities.

Expressions from jewels are not common in the ballads, except for the metaphor "jewel" applied affectionately to people.

> Ye've taken the timber out of my ain wood,
> And burnt my ain dear jewel.
> —*Lady Marjorie*, 77-78 (ii, 341).

> Ye're welcome, jewel, to your own.
> —*Young Beichan and Susie Pye*, 164 (iv, 9).

> Ye are my jewel.
> —*Blancheflour and Jellyflorice*, 85 (iv, 298).

> Cum well, cum wae, my jewels fair.
> —*Edom o' Gordon*, 63 (vi, 157).

Somewhat differently,

> Her comely eyes, like orient pearles.
> —*Fair Rosamond*, 11 (vii, 284).

Compare also the expression "silver-pearled deaw" already quoted.

And this good metaphor, once used:

> Seeking still for that pretious stone,
> The worde of trueth, so rare to find.
> —*The Duchess of Suffolk's Calamity*, 33-34 (vii, 300).

(β). We cannot better begin in this division than by introducing the reader to a pun, the first and perhaps the last he will meet in the course of the present investigation. The word "mettled" in the following quotation is originally metaphorical, mettle in the sense of spirit being the same word as "metal," temper of metal, etc.

> In manhood he's a mettled man,
> And a mettle-man by trade.
> —*Robin Hood and the Tinker*, 157-158 (v, 237).

Two figures from gold that do not seem to have an idea of colour are the following:

> Golden fame did thunder.
> —*The King of France's Daughter*, 176 (iv, 223);

and this rather better one:

> That he thought it to be but a meer golden dream.
> —*The Frolicsome Duke*, 56 (viii, 58).

Other solitary instances of comparisons with the mineral world are these:

> His skin more hard than brass was found.
> —*St. George and the Dragon*, 29 (i, 73).

> And all hir body lyke the lede.
> —*Thomas of Ersseldoune*, 96 (i, 102).

> It is your lady's heart's blood;
> 'Tis as clear as the lamer (amber).
> —*Lamkin*, 87–88 (iii, 98).

Summary.—The only figures of frequent occurrence under this head are the application of the word crystal to water and tears, and the metaphor *jewel* in addressing or speaking of beloved persons. Others, although they are not striking, are used too seldom to prove anything.

V.

Similes and Metaphors drawn from Fire and its Characteristics.

The qualities of fire have long been celebrated in popular simile. "Hot as fire," "red as fire," are customary expressions. In addition to this the brightness of fire is apparent to all. With obvious figures drawn from this last source, we will begin the discussion of f i r e similes.

> For the eyes that beene in his head
> They glister as doth the gleed.*
> —*King Arthur and Cornwall*, 110–111 (i, 236).

> As bright as fyre and brent
> —*Sir Cauline*, 148 (iii, 180).

(Percy's emendation of the folio line "harder than flyer, and brent");

> His armor glytteryde as dyd a glede.
> —*The Hunting of the Cheviot*, 57 (vii, 32).

> The moon shone like the gleed.
> —*Glenkindie*, 76 (ii, 12).

> When Thomas came before the king
> He glanced like the fire.
> —*Lord Thomas of Winesberry*, 43–44 (iv, 307).

* Gleed—A. S. Gléd—a burning coal.

The rapidity of movement in fire, and particularly in sparks, serves also for the foundation of several figures in the ballads.

> And then he will spring forth of his hand,
> As sparke dothe out of gleede.
> —*King Arthur and Cornwall*, 261-262 (i, 243).

> The Lindsays flew like fire about.
> —*The Battle of Otterbourne*, B, 115 (vii. 24).

The similarity of rumour to a raging flame is a common basis for simile and metaphor. In the ballads, this idea is apparent in the following:

> But lords and ladies blazed the fame.
> —*The Seven Champions*, 237 (i, 92).

And conversely,

> Whos prais sould not be smored (smothered).
> —*The Battle of Balrinnes*, 222 (vii, 226).

The spark, with its brilliant, short-lived existence, serves here as elsewhere for a figurative illustration of life itself.

> Nay spark o' life was there.
> —*The Lass of Lochroyan*, 144 (ii, 112).

The flame of love and the flame of anger are ideas known to all. They are used as follows in the popular poetry:

> Which set the lord's heart on fire.
> —*Patient Grissell*, 8 (iv, 208).

> The noble marquess in his heart felt such flame.
> —*Ibid.*, 19 (iv, 209).

> Till his heart was set on fire.
> —*The King of France's Daughter*, 151 (iv, 221).

> Long was his heart inflamed.
> —*Ibid.*, 158 (iv, 222).

> How oft she tried to drown the flame.
> —*The Hireman Chiel*, 60 (viii, 235).

> Save only Dido's boyling brest.
> —*Queen Dido*, 36 (viii, 209).

In the last, however, the idea is transferred from fire to its effect. More at length is the following variation of the same theme:

> But love is a durable fire,
>   In the mind ever burning ;
> Never sick, never dead, never cold,
>   From itself never turning.
> —*As I came from Walsingham*, 41-44 (iv, 194).

Perhaps the fore-runner, at all events the prototype, of Romeo's

> Love is a smoke raised with the fume of sighs,
> Cold fire, sick health, etc.

The **flame of anger** and of high courage, often akin to anger :

> Then Seaton started till his foot,
>   The fierce flame in his e'e.
> —*Lord Livingston*, 39-40 (iii, 344).

> Whose grisly looks and eyes like brands.
> —*Robin Hood and the Stranger*, 57 (v, 412).

> His een glittering for anger like a fiery gleed.
> —*The Fray of Suport*, 22 (vi, 117).

> But he was hail and het as fire.
> —*The Raid of Reidswire*, 38 (vi, 133).

> With wrath as hot as fire.
> —*The Wanton Wife of Bath*, 104 (viii, 156).

These two last similes are the only instances, so far as known, of the use in the ballads of the colloquial "hot as fire." The contrary "cold as ice" does not occur. Once more :

> But now as the knight in choler did burn.
> —*Sir Eglamore* 21 (viii, 197).

The idea of heat in wrath is too common to need further exploiting here. By way of contrast the cold of fear or depression may be introduced :

> Their hearts within them waxed cold.
> —*Samson*, 62 (viii, 203).

The value of the record demands the introduction at this point of the following bit of laboured verse, too puerile to be a production of the best ballad school:

> All which *incens'd* his lady so,
> She *burnt* with wrath extreame;
> At length the *fire* that long did *glow*,
> Burst forth into a *flame*.
> —*The Spanish Virgin*, 41–44 (iii, 362).

The accumulation of epithets here is worthy of a better cause.

The smoke of wrath is also expressed in the following hint of personification:

> Thoult see my sword with furie smoke.
> —*Robin Hood and the Farmer's Daughter*, 79 (v, 338).

Unclassified forms are these solitary instances:

> The battle grows hot on every side.
> —*Fragment*, 17 (v, 409).

> Joy shone within his face.
> —*Robin Hood and the Stranger*, 102 (v, 413).

[Shone like fire?]

> At every stroke he made him to smoke,
> As if he had been all on fire.
> —*Robin Hood and Little John*, 71–72 (v, 219).

The comparison of gold to a *burning mass* is also used, and for that reason is introduced here instead of under the chapter on colour-similes.

> Twa heads. . . .
> Lady Maisry's like the mo'ten goud.
> —*Lord Wa' Yates and Auld Ingram*, 111 (ii, 330).

> And mantel of the burning goud.
> —*Young Waters*, 11 (iii, 89).

And, finally, there may be a suggestion of simile in the epithet *red-hot* in the following, although it is probable the author had no such intent:

> A red-hot gad o' airn.
> —*The Young Tamlane*, 106 (i, 122).

Summary.—The figures, then, from the domain of fire, that seem to belong indisputably to the British popular mind, are such as arise from the brightness and rapidity of flame and sparks—" glittering like the gleed," "flies as doth the spark," etc.; and by metaphor, the flame of nature is transferred to the flame of love or the passion of anger. These figures are surely one indication of the popular origin of any poem, and as such are offered here without reserve.

B.

SIMILE AND METAPHOR DRAWN FROM ANIMALS AND THEIR CHARACTERISTICS.

The figures in this domain will be found, for all practical purposes, to fall under the same general description as those in the preceding division of the subject. They are obvious and such as would appeal to one who looked at nature objectively. There is no severe attempt, as in the great poets, to fit phenomena into a definition and scheme of life. For the balladists, the animals exist with certain strong appetites and habits, and from mere surface traits the figures are drawn. There is no subjection of animal life to man; in other words, no evidence in the ballads of Man Thinking. The similes shew the stronger, less attractive side of what may be called the animal character; to cite one case in several, "dog" is used throughout only in a contemptuous sense, with no recognition, apparently, of the animal's nobler qualities.

Having acknowledged this fact, there is no difficulty in classifying the figures. For the purposes of the present paper, the similes and metaphors derived from animals and their characteristics may be divided as follows:

    I. Similes and Metaphors drawn from Quadruped Life.
    II. Similes and Metaphors drawn from Bird Life.
    III. Similes and Metaphors drawn from Creeping Things and Things that Live in the Water.
    IV. Similes and Metaphors drawn from Insect Life.

The first of these divisions will be found to yield the most fruitful results, and the fourth the most meagre; but this is, perhaps, from the nature of the subject, inevitable.

I.

Similes and Metaphors drawn from Quadruped Life.

The figures in this subdivision represent
(a) The better qualities of strength and courage, and of lightness and grace;
(β) The meaner qualities that excite the contempt of man.
(γ) Miscellaneous qualities.

All will be found to fall under these heads, and under these heads they will now be taken up in order. It may be remarked once more, that there is no effort from first to last, on the part of the balladists, to pourtray sympathetically and with understanding the motives of animal life.

(a) The great examples of strength seem always to have been the boar, the lion, and the tiger; and the English bards, true to tradition, although they knew nothing of some of the animals in question, have preserved the similes derived therefrom, in their works. The following group needs no comment:

> They buckled then together so,
> Like two wild boars rashing.
> —*Sir Lancelot du Lake*, 109-110 (i, 60).

> Then Robin raged like a wild boar.
> —*Robin Hood and the Tanner*, 69 (v, 226).

> And about and about and about they went
> Like two wild boars in a chase.
> —*Ibid.*, 73-74 (v, 226).

> Like two wild boars so fierce.
> —*The Dragon of Wantley*, 123 (viii, 133).

> Like lions mov'd they laid on load.
> —*Chevy Chace*, 123 (vii, 48).

> As lyounes does poore lambes devoure,
> With bloodie teethe and naillis.
> —*The Battle of Balrinnes*, 101-102 (vii, 222).

> The M'Gregors fought like lyons bold.
> —*Bonny John Seton*, 45 (vii, 237).

> And with her husband thus they past,
> Like lambs beset with tygers wild.
> —*Thomas Stukeley*, 129-130 (vii, 303).

> And rid up as fierce as tygers.
> —*The Reading Skirmish*, 45 (vii, 245).

The following solitary instances occur:

> But Ethert Lunn, a baited bear,
> Had many battles seen.
> —*Auld Maitland*, 193-194 (vi, 228).

> Like to a wolf to worried be.
> —*Macpherson's Rant*, 11 (vi, 207).

The lightness and grace of d e e r , etc., are the next subject for discussion; and here we find many ballad examples in proof.

> Lyk hartes, up howes and hillis thei ranne.
> —*The Battle of Balrinés*, 289 (vii, 229).

> For she is wel shapyn, as lizt as a ra.
> —*The Turnament of Tottenham*, 129 (viii, 110).

> Like wounded harts chas'd all the day.
> —*Armstrong and Musgrave*, 62 (viii, 244).

> The deer that ye hae hunted lang,
> Then Hobie Noble is that deer!
> —*Hobie Noble*, 55-57 (vi, 101).

> This Frenshe com to Flaundres so liht so the hare.
> —*The Flemish Insurrection*, 81 (vi, 272).

In this connexion perhaps we may introduce:

> Herof habbeth the Flemyishe suithe god game.
> —*Ibid.*, 125.

(*β*) The meaner qualities of animals are generally summed up, in the ballads, in the words s w i n e , d o g , and a s s . The first of these is very frequently found to express drunkenness, and suggests the antiquity of the salient slang usage of to-day.

> Until they were a' deadly drunk
> As any wild-wood swine.
> —*Fause Goodrage*, 63-64 (iii, 43).

> Till she got him as deadly drunk
> As ony unhallowed swine.
> —*Young Hunting*, 39–40 (iii, 296).

Another familiar use is the following:

> Then sleep and snore like ony sow.
> —*Earl Richard* (B) 180 (iii, 278).

Observe, too, this group of similes:

> She's laid him on a dressing-table
> And stickit him like a swine.
> —*Hugh of Lincoln*, 27–28 (iii, 139).

And in a similar expression in a different version of the same ballad:

> And dress'd him like a swine.
> —*Sir Hugh*, 82 (iii, 143).

Again,

> Hue leyyen y the stretes, ystyked ase sywn.
> —*The Flemish Insurrection*, 42 (vi, 271).

The impression derived from the ballad similes and metaphors from d o g s is similar. The showing, besides, is large.

> That ye drew up wi' an English dog.
> —*Lady Maisry*, 55 (ii, 82).

> That have trepan'd our kind Scotchman,
> Like dogs to ding them down.
> —*The Enchanted Ring*, 27–28 (iii, 54).

> This dog's death I'm to die.
> —*The Queen's Marie*, 96 (iii, 119).

> 'Mong Noroway dogs no more.
> —*Sir Patrick Spens*, 68 (iii, 340).

> Hunted and drove before 'um like dogs.
> —*The Reading Skirmish*, 58 (vii, 246).

> Have you any more of your English dogs
> You want for to have slain?
> —*Johnie Scot*, 177–178 (iv, 50).

> The English dogs were cunning rogues.
> —*Lang Johnny Moir*, 33 (iv, 273).

> He'll loose yon bluidhound Borderers.
> —*The Outlaw Murray*, 255 (vi, 34).

The last is a better usage, however, and carries no idea of contempt. As much cannot be said for the following:

> It shall never be said we were hang'd like dogs.
> —*Johnie Armstrong*, 59 (vi, 43).

> I'm but like a forfoughen hound,
> Has been fighting in a syke [ditch].
> —*Hobie Noble*, 111–112 (vi, 104).

> Some Highland rogues, like hungry dogs.
> —*The Battle of Tranent Muir*, 97 (vii, 172).

> We'll pay thee at the nearest tree,
> Where we will hang thee like a hound.
> —*The Death of Parcy Reed*, 114 (vi, 145).

> Like unto dogs he'll cause you die.
> —*Billie Archie*, 28 (vi, 95).

> The black Baillie, that auld dog.
> —*The Battle of Alford*, 5 (vii, 238),

and frequently *dog* is contemptuously used. Compare in "As You Like It," Adam's "Is old dog my reward? Most true, I have lost my teeth in your service," and Shylock's

> You call me misbeliever, cut-throat dog.
> —*M. of V.*, i, 3.

Once, at least, in the ballads, the fighting qualities of a dog are specified in contradistinction to the mass of evidence above:

> But it was now too late to fear,
> For now it was come to fight dog, fight bear.
> —*Sir Eglamore*, 17–18 (viii, 197).

As often in modern English, moreover, so in the popular song, the term a s s is applied with a contemptuous, though not necessarily unkind, signification. The former feeling, however, often predominates, to the exclusion of anything else.

> Quoth bold Robbin Hood, "Thou dost prate like an ass."
> —*Robin Hood and Little John*, 83 (v, 218).

> And Robbin was, methinks, an asse.
> —*A True Tale of Robin Hood*, 383 (v, 368).

> Why, then, thou drunken ass.
> —*The Wanton Wife of Bath*, 35 (viii, 154).

(γ) To conclude, beasts are referred to in various scattered instances in a variety of ways. Collectively, they are used in these two similes:

> And now they renne away fro me
> As beastes on a row.
> —*A Little Geste of Robin Hood*, 237-238 (v, 55).

> Chessit lyke deirs* into their dens.
> —*The Battle of Harlaw*, 183 (vii, 188).

The characteristic of beasts is also referred to, without doubt, in the following personification:

> For a cannon's *roar*, etc.
> —*Bonny John Seton*, 59 (vii. 234),

and in

> The rest, they did quack and *roar*.
> —*Willie Wallace*, 72 (vi. 235).

The f o x, too, once serves as an illustration for cunning:

> The friar was as glad as a fox in his nest.
> —*The Friar in the Well*, 12 (viii, 122);

while in one poem for a special case we find

> You would have thought him for to be
> Some Egyptian porcupig.
> —*The Dragon of Wantley*, 83-84 (viii, 181);

and on the same page (ll. 87-88),

> they took him to be
> Some strange outlandish hedgehog.

The enumeration may be finished with these figures:

> But bring me, like a wand'ring sheep,
> Into thy fold again.
> —*The Wanton Wife of Bath*, 123-124 (viii, 157),

which, from its obvious origin, perhaps needs no introduction here; the concealed metaphor in

> But in all haste up to us they *flocked*.
> —*The Reading Skirmish*, 50 (vii, 246);

---

* A. S. dēor, animal. Cf. King Lear—Mice and rats and such small deer.

and, finally, the "yoke" of Cupid seems to apply to the receiver as to an animal in

> Yet fancy bids thee not to fear
> Which fetter'd thee in Cupid's yoke.
> —*Sir Eglamore*, 63–64 (viii, 210).

Such figures as the following hardly count in a general estimate of ballad figures. They are special instances, used only once; yet they are interesting as showing the sources from which ballad similes are drawn. These to be quoted are all common enough as sources of figure, except, odd as it may appear, the bull:

> His head is like unto a bull,
> His nose is like a boar.
> —*Queen Eleanor's Confession*, 69–70 (vi, 212).

> He's headed like a buck, she said,
> And backed like a boar.
> —*Ibid.*, ll. 73–74.

The same remarks apply to the following:

> His life was like a barrow-hogge
> Or like a filthy heap of dung.
> —*Gernutus the Jew of Venice*, 9, 13 (viii, 471).

Summary.—The figures most frequent in this first division of B, I, are those that refer to the resemblance between the warlike qualities of men and the rage of boars, lions, and tigers, in the order named; and those that found similes on the lightness and agility of deer. In the second division the epithets swine, dog, and ass are contemptuously applied to men. With these exceptions (themselves common enough) the figures are sporadic and of such a nature as to preclude classification.

II.

Similes and Metaphors drawn from Bird Life.

This division will be found to contain some of the happiest figures in the ballads. As was remarked somewhat earlier, the bright life of the country and the woodland finds frequent chronicle in the English and Scotch popular songs; and no feature of that life is more noticeable than the flight and song of birds. This feature, then, is often mentioned, and usually in a way to rivet the attention. "As blythe as bird on tree" is a common simile in our poems; and the allusion shows a careful study of nature in its gayest moods. "The gay goss-hawk" is also much in evidence. These figures will now be taken up in detail.

As for the song and "blitheness" of birds we find the following group of figures in the ballads:

> As blythe as ony bird on tree.
> —*The Laird of Waristoun*, 16 (lii, 319).

> As blythe's a bird on tree.
> —*Blancheflour and Jellyflorice*, 10 (iv, 295).

> Nae bird on the brier e'er sang sae clear
> As the young knight and his ladie.
> —*Geordie* (B), 31–32 (viii, 97).

> The bird never sang mair sweet on the bush
> Nor the knight sung at the baking.
> —*The Duke of Athol's Nurse*, 55–56 (viii, 230).

> The bird in the bush sung not so sweet
> As sung this bonny lady.
> —*The Rantin' Laddie*, 95–96 (iv, 101).

The swiftness of birds is attested by some very good similes.

> And he's gone skipping down the stair,
> Swift as the bird that flaw.
> —*The Hireman Chiel*, 31–32 (viii, 234).

> He has gone whistling o'er the knowe,
> Swift as the bird that flaw.
> —*The Hireman Chiel*, 192–193 (viii, 240).

Once, at least, the "swift" bird is specified:

> When the Italian, like a swallow swift
> Owre Johnie's head did flee.
> —*Johnie Scot*, 161–162 (iv, 58).

The flight of birds in fear, again, is the foundation of at least one simile:

> And dinna flee like a frighted bird
> That's chased frae its nest i' the morning.
> —*Johnie Cope*, 11–12 (vii, 274),

where there is evidence, in the last line, of the individual poet working in fields not common to the general balladist.

The "gay" goss-hawk also serves its turn in popular poetry; frequently it has the added idea of wildness.

> The boy stared wild, like a gray goss-hawk.
> —*Fause Goodrage*, 121 (iii, 45).

And in the same poem the father addresses his son by the title in question:

> And ye must learn, my gay goss-hawk.
> —*Ibid.*, l. 89.

Differently,
> He mewde hir up as men mew hawkes.
> —*The Taming of a Shrew*, 87 (viii, 185).

Once, too, a father speaks of his son as a cock:

> My gude house-cock, my only son.
> —*Willie and Maisry*, 46 (li, 59).

The gentleness of the dove is proverbial and was a common illustration with the ballad writers. It is usual to call a person of such character a "turtle-dove." One example will suffice:

> And sae has he the turtle-dow
> With the truth o' his wild hand.
> —*Fause Goodrage*, 139–140 (iii, 46).

Again in the same poem we find "your turtle-dow" (your daughter.)

Coming to more direct similes under this head, two shining instances arrest the attention:

> In vain in humble sort she strove
>   Her fury to disarm;
> As well the weakness of the dove,
>   The bloody hawke might charm.
> —*The Spanish Virgin*, 29–32 (iii, 361).

> The bonny dew likes na its mate
> .   .   .   .   .
> Better, my dearest Chil Ether,
> Than Maisry loves her brither.
> —*Chil Ether*, 9–12 (iv, 299).

There is a distinctly subjective tone to these similes; a tone that is quite apparent in the following extract:

> The linnet is a bonnie bird,
> And aften flees far frae its nest;
> So all the world may plainly see,
> They're far awa that I love best.
> —*Lord Jamie Douglas*, 125-128 (iv, 142).

The grim humour of the next quotation is not bad :

> The egg is chipp'd, the bird is flown,
> Ye'll see na mair o' young Logie.
> —*The Laird o' Logie*, 67-68 (iv, 113).

But most beautiful of all—somewhat too beautiful—is the solitary reference to the habit of the swan :

> And sing, like a swan, my doom.
> —*The Damosel's Complaint*, 52 (ii, 386);

with which we may compare Shakspere's

> He makes a swan-like end, fading in music.
> —*M. of V.* iii, 2, 44-45,

and Tennyson's

> Like some full-breasted swan
> That fluting a wild carol ere her death.

Solitary instances that lack corroboration in other ballads are such as the following:

> His berd was syde ay large span
> And glided als the fether of pae (peacock).
> —*Als I Yod on Ay Mounday*, 19-20 (i, 274).

Similarly, from the habits of the same bird,

> I spread my plumes, as wantons do.
> —*Jane Shore*, 21 (vii, 195).

The flight of birds is undoubtedly the foundation of

> And they loot off a flight of arrows.
> —*The Raid of Reidswire*, 72 (vi, 130);

and in the following, the joining of a certain useful fowl with beasts of magnitude is funny:

> The rest they did *quack* an' roar.
> — *Willie Wallace*, 72 (vi, 235).

The next is decidedly humorous:

> For houses and churches were to him geese and turkies.
> —*The Dragon of Wantley* (viii, 129).

Finally,

> Hue were laht* by the net, so bryd is in snare.
> —*The Flemish Insurrection*, 83 (vi, 272).

The birds, once more, are the basis of the metaphor

> This in our hearts we freely did hatch.
> —*The Reading Skirmish*, 27 (vii, 245);

and once, to twilight or dawn, is applied the striking metaphor,

> The dun feather and gray.
> —*Reedisdale and Wise William*, 32 (viii, 89).

Summary.—The commonest similes, then, drawn from bird life are those that refer to the bird's joyousness, song, and flight. These occur again and again, and are surely proofs of the popular origin of any ballad. Less frequent allusion is made to the goss-hawk and turtle-dove (mostly as metaphors). Other figures are too rare to be classified, and three, at least, show a subjective force and a beauty that are indisputable evidence of their authors' individuality. Altogether, the bird similes are perhaps the best and happiest in the ballads.

III.

Similes and Metaphors drawn from Creeping Things and Things that Live in the Water.

These figures are not numerous, and may be summed up in a few words. They lack originality and are such as suggest themselves to the dullest intellect. They occupy but a minimum space in the aggregate of the figures in the ballads, and with few exceptions are used in particular cases where nothing else would do.

* Laht—caught.

One very fair instance that recalls Virgil's famous *latet anguis in herba* is the following:

> Thy fair words make me suspect thee,
> Serpents are where flowers grow.
> —*The Spanish Lady's Love*, 27-28 (iv, 203).

Reference is likewise made to the serpent in the metaphor

> " I have a secret to reveale,"
> She said, "my heart doth sting."
> —*The Gentleman in Thracia*, 51-52 (viii, 160).

And again, three times:

> Where fear and sting of conscience.
> —*George Barnwell*, 103 (viii, 226).

> Which did his heart with sorrow sting.
> —*St. George and the Dragon*, 57 (i, 75).

> Was forc'd the sting of death to feel.
> *Ibid.*, 204, 80.

Two other figures in this department are:

> Auld Ingram's [head] like a toad.
> —*Lord Wa' Yates*, etc. 112 (ii, 330).

> He stert up as a snayle.
> —*The Turnament of Tottenham*, 177 (viii, 112).

Regarding creatures that live in the water, we find

> When I come to a deep water,
> I can swim thro' like ony otter.
> —*Earl Richard* (B), 99-100 (iii, 270);

and on the same page,

> I can swim thro' like ony eel.

In a variant version of the same poem occur the lines:

> That I can soum this wan water
> Like a fish in a flude—
> . . . . .
> As though I was an otter.
> —*Earl Richard* (B), 29, 34 (iii, 306).

Summary.—The figures, then, in this subdivision will be seen to be too rare to admit of classification under a formula for ballad conduct. With the possible exception of the metaphorical use of *sting*, there is nothing that invites attention or suggests a settled usage on the part of the bards.

IV.

Similes drawn from Insect Life.

Coming to the final heading of animal life, we find two similes to support us in making such a division. They are as follows:

> I count him lighter than a flee.
> —*Jock o' the Side*, 92 (vi, 85);

to which may be compared Chaucer's "I count him not a flee," and the ballad

> They counted us not worth a louse.
> —*The Raid of the Reidswire*, 36 (vi, 133).

The second and better simile:

> And so they fled, wi' a' their main,
> Down ower the brae, like clogged bees.
> —*Raid of Reidswire*, 119–120.

To conclude, on this line, it will be seen how much less frequent in the ballads are figures drawn from animal life than those drawn from inanimate nature. With the exception of the bird-similes, again, they are less striking and less interesting than those under the first great division of the subject.

C.

SIMILE AND METAPHOR DRAWN FROM MAN AND HIS HABITS.

The figures in this division will be found to be much more numerous than in the preceding division of the subject, though not so numerous as the figures from the domain of nature. The general characteristics of these figures are again homeliness and simplicity. This aspect of the ballad figures cannot be insisted on too often. The similes and metaphors drawn from man and his habits are such as would most naturally appeal to an untrained intelligence seeking for resemblances between man and the workings of that intelligence. Of the subjective resemblance, however, there is little trace. The external characteristics of man, his form and bearing, the members of his body, etc., are used as bases for figures; his moral attributes are sparingly treated. Again, the products of man's ingenuity and inventive power serve as sources for figure, but they are mentioned by the way, with no working out of detail in the resemblances.

To put it more plainly, a man, in the ballads, is, perhaps, compared, from external traits only, to a king, or an angel, or a palmer; but seldom, if ever, is there a figure arising from a knowledge of man's moral nature. Never, for instance, do we find a figure such as the one already quoted from Coleridge, beginning

>Like one that on a lonesome road, etc.,

where the simile springs from a moral or intellectual, rather than a physical resemblance. A good example of ballad-simile under this head would be

>Earl Douglas on his milk-white steed,
>Most like a baron bold.
>—*Chevy Chace*, 65-66 (vii, 46),

where the resemblance is moral to a certain extent, but tinctured deeply by external showing.

For the sake of convenience, the figures in this section will be divided under four great heads:

I. Simile and Metaphor drawn from the Human Body.

II. Simile and Metaphor drawn from Man as Man, in Various Relations of Life.

III. Simile and Metaphor drawn from Man as a Moral and Intellectual Being.

IV. Simile and Metaphor drawn from the Life and Works of Man.

I.

Similes and Metaphors drawn from the Human Body.

The resemblances employed in this division are not many or striking, and may be summed up in a few words.

In Sir Andrew Barton 48 (vii, 58) we find the epithet h e a d twice used as a term for high rank.

> Of a hundred gunners to be the head.

This line occurs again, and a variation, likewise, in

> To be the head I have chosen thee.
> —*Ibid.*, 60 (vii, 59).

Once, too, the familiar epithet of the sun:

> But the all-seeing *eye* of heaven.
> —*The Gentleman in Thracia*, 37 (viii, 159).

A similar figure:

> Wi' that he vanish'd frae her sight,
> Wi' the twinkling o' an eye.
> —*The Courteous Knight*, 131-132 (viii, 277).

Once occurs the beautiful metaphor:

> Until they came to a broad river,
> An *arm* of a lonesome sea.
> —*May Colvin*, 19-20 (ii, 274).

For completeness, we include

> The Protestants of Drogheda
> . . . . .
> They being but a handful.
> —*The Boyne Water*, 49, 52 (vii, 255).

Figures derived from the senses of man are the following:

> We's be a *motte* into his sight,
> Or he pas hame againe.
> —*The Battle of Balrinnes*, 55-56 (vii, 220).

> To counsel this lady was *deaf*,
> To judgement she was *blind*.
> —*Fair Margaret of Craignargat*, 69-70 (vii, 252).

Another sense is called upon here:

> "Thou *smells* of a coward," said Robin Hood.
> —*Robin Hood and the Golden Arrow*, 41 (v, 385).

Compare Shakspere's

> O my offence is rank; it *smells* to heaven.
> —*Hamlet*, iii, 3, 37.

The sense of t a s t e is more fully represented:

> And after sought her lip to *taste*.
> —*Robin Hood and the Farmer's Daughter*, 15 (v, 335).

And, of a sound drubbing:

> He smil'd to see his merry young men
> Had gotten a taste of the tree.
> —*Robin Hood and the Beggar*, 253-254 (v, 203).

Again, with a change from a physical to a moral standpoint,

> To tast of that extremity.
> —*King of Scots*, etc., 63 (vii, 106).

Taste, once more, may be the foundation of

> Widdowes sweete comfort found.
> —*Whittington's Advancement*, 114 (viii, 171),

although we referred the epithet s w e e t in most cases to B, II, the discussion of figures from the plant world. Yet taste is, conversely, the source of

> Into a bitter passion he presently fell.
> —*Catskin's Garland*, 16 (viii, 173),

and undoubtedly of the familiar

> The cream of the jest.
> —*Ibid.*, 33.

The sense of t o u c h is called upon for

> To feel his coyne, his hands did itch.
> —*A True Ballad of Robin Hood*, 207 (v, 362),

to which we may compare Shakspere's

> you yourself
> Are much condemn'd to have an itching palm.
> —*Julius Cæsar*, iv, 3, 10.

The kindred muscular sense is also the inspiration of the following group of figures:

> Of comforte that was not colde.
> —*The Battle of Otterbourne*, 18 (vii, 7).

> "This is cold comfort," sais my lord.
> —*Sir Andrew Barton*, 117 (vii, 61).

> Then home rode the abbot of comfort so cold.
> —*King John and the Abbot of Canterbury*, 45 (viii, 8).

> I trow, quoth she, your courage is cooled.
> —*The Friar in the Well*, 47 (viii, 124).

The figure by which the heart in sorrow is likened to a wounded person, or a person that can be wounded, is represented several times in the ballads. These figures will be included here, although, very possibly, a better disposition of them could be suggested. They are as follows:

> And for his master's sad perille
> His very heart did bleed.
> —*Old Robin of Portingale*, 27-28 (iii, 35).

> If the damsel's eyes have pierc'd your heart.
> —*Robin Hood and the Stranger*, 37 (v, 413).

> But 'tis the poor distress'd princess
> That wounds me to the heart.
> —*Ibid.*, 91-92.

> When death had pierced the tender heart.
> —*Queen Dido*, 67, (viii, 210).

Similarly,
> For hym ther hartes were sore.
> —*The Battle of Otterbourne*, 142 (vii, 17).

Similarly, too, perhaps,
> Come, death, quoth she, resolve my smart.
> —*Queen Dido*, 65 (viii, 210);

and
> Their hearts were clogg'd with care.
> —*Armstrong and Musgrave*, 76 (viii, 246).

[Clogged, "surrounded by a mass or impediment. The substantive from the verb, not vice versâ." *Skeat*.]

Compare

> Thus were the knights both pricked in love.
> —*Ibid.*, 57 (viii, 245).

Applied to the mind:

> But nowe behold what wounded most my mind.
> —*Titus Andronicus*, 49 (viii, 191).

> For in his mind
> He bore the wounds of woe.
> —*King Lear and his Three Daughters*, 135–136 (vii, 281).

The two metaphors that follow may close the discussion. Of a lover occurs the line,

> Here lyes my sweete hart-roote.
> —*Old Robin of Portingale*, 104 (iii, 39);

and similarly, of the beloved:

> Wherefore, adew, my owne hert true.
> —*The Nutbrowne Maide*, 57 (iv, 146).

Summary.—It will be readily seen that it is impossible to lay down a positive rule for figures under this division. Similes and metaphors drawn from the sense of taste and from the muscular sense ("cold comfort"), are commoner than the others, and seem to have passed into a circulation real, though limited. The use of the "wounded heart" is almost commonplace; but this seems to be somewhat aside from the subject. One thing, however, may be said with certainty; the balladists frequently drew on the human body by way of illustration, but individual preference is more strongly marked here than in any preceding part of the subject, and consequently, within certain bounds, the evidences of the author's personality are more apparent than in the ballad commonplaces we are trying to prove. These evidences result in a freshness and a novelty found in no other department of the ballad figures.

II.

Similes and Metaphors drawn from Man as Man, in Various Relations of Life.

The figures under this head will, of course, admit of great variety. The callings of men are so numerous, that the field for illustration is almost unlimited. Hence, we shall see in the ballad figures resemblances drawn from man as king, as noble, as leader of armies and of men, as commoner, etc.; even, if you please, from what faith conceives man to be in another world. For the sake of convenience, then, man may be classified under the heavenly, the royal, the noble, and the common man, and under these four heads will be found the figures descriptive of his habits.

a. Man in his Celestial Aspect.

The figures here are of a uniform character, and extremely simple. A woman, for instance, is called an "angel," or some one is "heavenly;" the illustration goes no further.

> His bride followed after, *an angel* most bryght.
> —*The Blind Beggar's Daughter of Bednall Green*, 18 (iv, 168).

> And passing by, *like an angel bright*.
> —*The Fair Flower of Northumberland*, 13 (iv, 181).

> With *angel-like* face.
> —*As I came from Walsingham*, 14 (iv, 192).

> And as she, *like an angel bright*.
> —*Armstrong and Musgrave*, 113 (viii, 247).

> Beheld her *heavenly* face.
> —*Fair Rosamond*, 146 (vii, 289).

Somewhat differently,

> She much *like a goddess* drest in great array.
> —*Catskin's Garland*, 183 (viii, 180).

> She seemed so *divine*.
> —*George Barnwell*, 56 (viii, 215).

One solitary figure, though it can hardly be included here,

will be put among these, the supernatural figures, because it is too much alone to be formed into a separate class:

> And said it was *the fairy court*
> To see him in array.
> —*Katharine Janfarie*, 35–36 (iv, 31).

And, quite conversely,

> He stamped and stared, and awaye he ranne,
> As the *devill* had him borne.
> —*Edward IV. and the Tanner*, 127–128 (viii, 29);

and,

> And I kan nae thing she 'pear'd to be,
> But the *fiend* that wons in hell.
> —*King Henry*, 23–24 (i, 148.)

β. Man as King.

The figures here are more numerous than in the preceding subdivision, although still of a uniform character. It need scarcely be said that *man* is used generically throughout this essay.

> Was fine as ony queen.
> —*Tam-a-Line*, 42 (i, 259).

> But the youngest look'd like beauty's queen.
> —*The Cruel Brother*, 11 (ii, 252).

> Who like a queen did appear,
> In her gait, in her pace.
> —*As I Came from Walsingham*, 15–16 (iv, 192).

> The bride lookt like a queen.
> —*Robin Hood and Allin a Dale*, 106 (v, 283).

Similar use is made of the simile-adjective r o y a l:

> For all his *ryall* chere.
> —*A Little Geste of Robin Hood*, 102 (v, 66).

> There rydeth no bysshop in this londe
> So *ryally* I understond.
> —*Ibid.*, 47–48 (v, 82).

> There the king *royally*, in princely majestie.
> —*The King and the Miller of Mansfield*, 79 (viii, 42).

> Full *royally* hee welcomed them home.*
> —*Sir Andrew Barton*, 294 (Folio, iii, 417).

---

* Percy Rel.   King Henry's grace, with *royall* cheere
Welcomed the noble Howard Home, 157–158 (vii, 69).

Princely is also used in the later ballads:

> With *princely* power and peace.
> —*King Lear*, 2 (vii, 276).

> So *princely* seeming beautiful.
> —*Ibid.*, 7 (vii, 277).

> A faire and *princely* dame.
> —*Fair Rosamond*, 4 (vii, 284).

> Full oft betweene his *princely* armes.
> —*Ibid.*, 79.

γ. Man as Noble, etc.

In the division of man as ennobled and occupying positions of trust we find figures of the same simplicity and directness.

> Earl Douglas on a milk-white steed,
> Most *like a baron bold.*
> —*Chevy Chace*, 65–66 (vii, 46).

> At last these two stout earls did meet,
> *Like captains* of great might.
> —*Ibid.*, 121–122.

And, corresponding to princely, the adjective lordly:

> The king replied fu' *lordly.*
> —*Geordie*, 38 (viii, 95).

δ. Man in Various Conditions of Life.

In this subdivision will be found, very naturally, a number of comparisons drawn from varied sources. No attempt will be made to classify them, as in many cases they occur but once in the ballads. Some of these are the following:

> And *like a palmer* dyed I.
> —*Legend of Sir Guy*, 131 (i, 68).

> *Like to a fryer*, bold Robin Hood,
> Was accoutred in his array.
> —*Robin Hood's Golden Prize*, 9–10 (v, 304).

> All cladd in gray, in *pilgrim* sort.
> —*Legend of Sir Guy*, 65 (i, 66).

Sporadic examples are these:

> And *like a soldier* buried gallantly.
> —*Thomas Stukeley*, 135 (vii, 312).

> Had entertainment *like to gentlemen.*
> —*Ibid.*, 75.

> Nay rather let me, *like a page*,
> Your sword and target beare.
> —*Fair Rosamond*, 93–94 (vii, 287).

> Nor be abusit *lyk a slaif*.
> —*The Battle of Harlaw*, 39 (vii, 183).

Two rather more extended conceptions should be quoted:

> No greater *thief* lies hidden under skies,
> Than beauty closely lodgde in womens eyes.
> —*In Sherwood Livde Stout Robin Hood*, 14–15 (v, 433).

> And as oftentimes he greets you well,
> as any harte can thinke,
> or *schoolmasters in any schoole*,
> wryting with pen & inke.
> —*Child Maurice, Folio*, 47–50 (ii, 503).

The images drawn from the appearance of women are not numerous:

> In troth ye sit *like ony bride*.
> —*Jock o' the Side*, 100 (vi, 86).

> So *like an old witch* looks she.
> —*Robin Hood and the Bishop*, 48 (v, 300).

> His wife, *like Maid Marian*, did mince at that tide.
> —*The King and the Miller of Mansfield*, 60 (viii, 41);

and this peculiar one:

> *like to the queen of spades*
> The millers wife did soe orderly stand,
> A *milk-maids courtesye* at every word.
> —*Ibid.*, 75–77.

Summary.—Man as man, in various relations, serves, then, as the basis for many common figures. "Like an angel," "heavenly," "royal," "princely," "like a queen" (nowhere "like a king"), are very frequently used. Other comparisons from varied sources appear, and of uniform simplicity, but they do not admit of satisfactory classification.

III.

Similes and Metaphors drawn from Man as a Moral and Intellectual Being.

The most frequent figures in this division are, naturally enough, those that arise from man's fighting qualities; for, the balladist flourishing when chivalry was at its height,* and later, when border warfare was rife, would be most of all impressed with these qualities of virility and strength. The gentler virtues of man are never called upon to supply resemblances in thought. As might be expected, these qualities would not appeal to a rude minstrel, and it is only the "clerkly" poet that could leap to such a lofty sentiment as Emilia's

> Thou hast not half that power to do me harm
> As I have to be hurt.

An essentially feminine mind such as Bulwer's might see the superiority of the pen over the sword, or, in fact, of any gentle art over the martial spirit, but the true balladist, like his northern prototype, the Skald, delights in blood and the clang of arms. In these things he revels and he draws thence, as from the chief source of his inspiration, the figures based on the moral and intellectual character of man.

Let us, then, begin with this aspect of the case. The m a d - n e s s of true and transcendent courage is familiar to all; it is likewise, in the ballads, the most frequent sign of valour. To quote:

> Up then sterte good Robyn
> As a man that had be wode.†
> —*A Little Geste of Robin Hood*, 93-94 (v, 103).

> And raved like one that's mad,
> So we'll leave him chafing in his grease.
> —*Robin Hood and the Golden Arrow*, 128-129 (v, 388).

> Then they fought on like mad men all.
> —*Johnie Armstrong*, 73 (vi, 44).

---

* See Percy. Essay on the Ancient Minstrels in England, prefixed to the Reliques.

† Wode. A. S. wód, mad.

> Then like a mad man Jonne laide about,
> And like a mad man then fought hee.
> —*Johnie Armstrong*, 57–58 (vi, 253) ;

and,

> The Camerons scow'r'd, as they were mad.
> —*Will Lickladle*, etc., 89 (vii, 263).

It may be as well, perhaps, to include in this list of the similes of madness, the few cases where there is no idea of courage, in which, possibly, there may be just the contrary notion:

> When shee had taken the mantle,
> She stoode as shee had beene madd.
> —*The Boy and the Mantle*, (i, 9).

> They ran as they wer wode.
> —*Robin Hood and the Potter*, 260 (v, 29).

But, after all, the great manifestation or promise of courage is manliness; and it is exclusively of this quality of courage that the expression m a n l y (manlic—manlike) is used in the ballads.

> We will fight it out most *manfully*.
> —*Johnie Armstrong*, 60 (vi, 43).

> Withstood the Greekes in *manfull* wise.
> —*Queen Dido*, 2 (viii, 207).

> But Gardner brave did still behave
> *Like to a hero bright*, man.
> —*The Battle of Tranent-Muir*, 57–58 (vii, 171).

The same idea is apparent in

> When we attack like Highland trews.
> —*The Battle of Sheriff-Muir*, 72 (vii, 262),

and in

> But More of More Hall
> Like a valiant son of Mars.
> —*The Dragon of Wantley*, 133–134 (viii, 133).

And underlying the following metaphor is the same notion of martial spirit:

> I hold my life a mortal fo.
> —*The Merchant's Daughter*, etc., 24 (iv, 329).

In contradistinction to the conception of courage we have that of cowardice. "Thou smells of a coward" has already been noted. Compare

> Thou talk'st like a coward.
> —*Robin Hood and Little John*, 37 (v, 218).

> The master with the bullie's face,
> And with the coward's heart, man.
> —*Huntley's Retreat*, 36 (vii, 270);

and, slightly different,

> To act a traitor's part, man.
> —*Ibid.*, 36.

Next to valour, in the age of chivalry, came the domestic affections. These affections are the source, in the ballads, of a few similes which will here be noted. The most frequent is that of fraternal love.

> And thus the night they a' hae spent,
> Just as they had been brither and brither.
> —*Jock o' the Side*, 147–148 (vi, 88).

> They sat them down upon one seat,
> Like loving brethren dear.
> —*Armstrong and Musgrave*, 17–18 (viii, 244);

and in this satirical line of a desertion:

> He, brother-like, did quit his ground.
> —*Huntley's Retreat*, 71 (vii, 271).

There is little else in this field of inspiration, so fruitful to the modern poet. The pathos of the ballads comes from story and situation; never from the allusion to domestic ties and tender associations that poets like Burns and Longfellow have used so extensively. The few touches that remain will now be taken up in order. The following are the references to the life of childhood:

> For love is a careless child
> And forgets promise past;
> He is blind, he is deaf, when he list,
> And in faith never fast.
> . . . . . .
> He is won with a word of despair
> And is lost with a toy.
> —*As I Come from Walsingham*, 29–36 (iv, 193);

and in the same description we have woman's love

> Under which many *childish* desires.

Again:

> For bonny doo loves na its mate,
> *Nor babe at breast its mither*,
> Better, my dearest Chil Ether,
> Than Maisry loves her brither.
> —*Chil Ether*, 9-12 (iv, 299).

Friendship is once called upon to supply a figure, in the following, where the peddler's pack partially saved him from the arrow:

> Though the packe did stand his friend.
> —*Robin Hood and the Peddlers*, 52 (v, 245).

Scattered instances are these:

> He pressede to pull frowte with his hande,
> Als man for fude that was nere faynt.
> —*Thomas of Ersseldoune*, 131-132 (i, 103).

> And at one sup he eat them up,
> As one would eat an apple.
> —*The Dragon of Wantley*, 23-24 (viii, 129).

> "Robin," said he, "I'll now tell thee
> The very *naked* truth."
> —*The King's Disguise*, 119-120 (v, 380),

where truth is compared to a naked man or child, since truth is as defenceless against investigation as a naked man against attack. Opposed to this, man's clothing furnishes the following figure:

> The lift * *was clothed* with cloudis gray,
> And *owermaskit* was the moone.
> —*The Battle of Balrinnes*, 5-6 (vii, 218).

Also,

> And *cloke* no cause for ill nor good.
> —*The Raid of the Reidswire*, 66 (vii, 134).

The household shelter is, likewise, the basis of the figure in *lodged* in

> Than beauty closely *lodgde* in womens eyes.
> —*In Sherwood Livde Stout Robin Hood*, 15 (v, 433).

---

* Air. Icelandic, lopt; German, luft.

Similarly, the metaphor "quarter:"

> The three that remain'd call'd to Robin for *quarter.*
> —*Robin Hood's Birth*, etc., 169 (v, 350).

Habits of men are instanced in several scattered examples:

> And thus, as one being in a trance.
> —*Queen Dido*, 133 (viii, 212).

> And is not to be given away
> But *as* jewels are bought and sold.
> —*The Northern Lord*, 10-11 (viii, 278).

> Farewell, my dear, and chiefest *treasure* of my heart.
> —*The Merchant's Daughter*, etc., 18 (iv, 329).

There is probably a radical metaphor here:

> In merry Shirwood he *spends* his dayes.
> —*Robin Hood and His Huntes-Men*, 11 (v, 435),

and in

> Thus *spending* of her time away.
> —*The Gentleman in Thracia*, 33 (viii, 159).

To conclude, the following may be cited of a fight:

> sayes, I will ordain them such a *breake-fast*
> as was not in the North this 1000 yeere.
> —*Rising in the North*, 143-144 (Folio ii, 215).

Man's religious habits are, perhaps, the foundation of the following, although such idea may have left the word "sacrifice" before it was used here:

> Who fell a bleeding *sacrifice*
> To this fierce giant's rage.
> —*The Seven Champions*, 159-160 (i, 89).

Pathos, finally, is not lacking in

> Left to the warld thair *last gude-nicht.*
> —*The Battle of Harlaw*, 232 (vii, 189).

Summary.—Under the moral aspect of man, the figures assuredly admit of classification. The madness of courage or anger is common enough in the ballads to pass unquestioned. Fraternal affection and the life of children are less frequently in evidence, but both occur more than once. Under the head of man's habits we find several references to his commercial life. "*Spending* one's time," " as jewels are bought and sold." The other facts of daily life are more sparingly used, but the few mentioned here are certainly common enough to pass unchallenged.

IV.

Similes and Metaphors drawn from the Life and Works of Man.

The figures will again be found, in this division, to be of the simplest description, derived from the homely, everyday pursuits of men. There are references to agriculture, to navigation, and other prosaic occupations, and also allusions to the more primitive inventions of our fathers. There are, as well, explicit references to the lighter avocations and sports of life, and these will be included under this head. For convenience, the subject will be divided into

(*a.*) Simile and Metaphor drawn from Man's Vocation;
(*β.*) Simile and Metaphor drawn from Man's Invention;
(*γ.*) Simile and Metaphor drawn from Man's Avocation.

(*a.*) Simile and Metaphor drawn from Man's Vocation.

The figures here are such as would be expected from an early people before the introduction of machinery and its accompanying refinements. These figures are drawn from many sources, and none is so common as to degenerate into a class.

The three following comparisons to agricultural pursuits of a man laying blows about him may be classed together:

> Then to it each goes, and follow'd their blows,
> As if they had been threshing of corn.
> —*Robin Hood and Little John*, 63-64 (v, 219).

> Then Bland was in hast, he laid on so fast,
> As though he had been cleaving of wood.
> —*Robin Hood and The Tanner*, 71-72 (v, 226).

> They brittened tham [the roes] als they were wode.
> —*Thomas of Ersseldoune*, 201 (i, 106),

although it is possible that this brittening or carving was done as if they were "mad," not as if the victims were "wood."

In Robin Hood and The Tanner, the latter's calling is made to do service for several bits of slangy metaphor.

> I will *tan* thy hide for nought.
> —*Robin Hood and The Tanner*, 96 (v, 227).

> He is a bonny blade, and master of his trade,
> For soundly he hath *tan'd* my hide.
> —*Ibid.*, 122-123.

> And he shall *tan* my hide, too.
> —*Ibid.*, 127.

And it may be remarked, in passing, that the balladist, like the poet, if he says a thing that pleases him, is apt to repeat it as often as possible. All poetry is filled with instances of novel metres, phrases, and ideas repeated as soon as decorum will allow, by their apparently delighted authors.

Another useful pursuit is typified in the following naïve description of a fight:

> Ane bloodie *broust* * there was *brouine*.
> —*The Battle of Balrinnes*, 14 (vii, 218).

Cooking is called upon in

> They hew'd him when they had him got,
> As small as flesh into the pot.
> —*Armstrong and Musgrave*, 149-150 (viii, 248).

> She would meal you with millering,
> That she gathers at the mill,
> And mak you thick as any daigh (dough).
> —*Earl Richard*, 173-175 (iii, 273);

and,

> While others took flight, being *raw*, man.
> —*The Battle of Sheriff-Muir*, 10 (vii, 157).

Agriculture is the source of

> Yet *reapt* disgrace at my returning home.
> —*Titus Andronicus*, 4 (viii, 189),

and navigation of the next two:

> His weary course he *steers*
> Till fortune blessed him with a smile.
> —*The Seven Champions*, 174-175 (i, 90).

* Broust—brewing.

> Looke that your brydle be wight, my lord,
> And your horse goe swift as shipp at sea.*
> —*Northumberland Betrayed*, 209-210 (vii, 102).

A series of metaphors from the transferred meaning of *scour* may be introduced here, although the balladist, beyond doubt, had no idea of figure when he used them.

> In less than an hour, we [are] forcéd to scoure.
> —*The Reading Skirmish*, 31 (vii, 245).
>
> While Papists did scour from Protestant power.
> —*Undaunted Londonderry*, 55 (vii, 250).
>
> The Camerons scow'r'd as they were mad.
> —*The Battle of Sheriff-Muir*, 89 (vii, 263).

And similarly,

> With borderers *pricking* hither and thither.
> —*Rookhope Ryde*, 22 (vi, 123).

This branch of the subject may be left with pointing out that the last body of figures is again from a particular related group of ballads; a result that has been noted in other instances.

(β.) Simile and Metaphor drawn from Man's Invention.

Here we find reference to many useful, if not ornamental, devices of man. Once, of self-remorse, we find

> And alace my ain *wand dings* me now.
> —*Lord Jamie Douglas*, 16 (iv, 137).

Similarly,

> Thou shalt be the *staff* of my age.
> —*Robin Hood's Birth*, etc., 86 (v, 346).
>
> With a sting in his tayl as long as a *flayl*.
> —*The Dragon of Wantley*, 11 (viii, 128).

Again, of magical machinations:

> fairly freed
> From the enchanted heavy *yoke*.
> —*The Seven Champions*, 118-119 (i, 88).
>
> "I am a poor fisherman," said he then,
> "This day *intrapped* all in care."
> —*The Noble Fisherman*, 23-24 (v, 330).

---

* Percy's wording. The Folio MS. reads (ii, 225, 200):
> That you may go as a shipp at sea.

> [Jealousy] is the devil's *snare*.
> —*The Spanish Virgin*, 128 (iii, 365).

> I would hae *lockt* my hert *wi'* a *key o' gowd*,
> And *pinned* it *wi'* a *siller pin*.
> —*Lord Jamie Douglas*, 23-24 (iv, 137).

> I've lost my hopes, I've lost my joy,
> I've lost the *key* but and the *lock* (*i.e.* my son).
> —*Graeme and Bewick*, 167-168 (iii, 85).

Another group is interesting as showing the lesser, more domestic life of man:

> It was from the top to the toe,
> As sheeres had itt ahread.
> —*The Boy and the Mantle*, 39-40 (i, 9).

> And shin'd like candles bright.
> —*Lord Livingston*, 26 (iii, 344).

> Delay not time, thy *glass* is run.
> —*Queen Dido*, 113 (viii, 211),

where life is compared to the hour-glass.

> And her skin was as smooth as glass.
> —*Robin Hood's Birth, etc.*, 114 (v, 347).

> On four-half to honge, huere myrour to be.
> —*The Execution of Sir Simon Fraser*, 27 (vi, 275).

> When he these lines full fraught with gall,
> Perused had and *wayed* them right.
> —*Queen Dido*, 97-98 (viii, 211).

And this humorous description of a scold:

> But still her tongue on pattens ran.
> —*The Taming of a Shrew*, 79 (viii, 185).

The bell—one of the most familiar of local sounds—is used a few times in comparisons:

> The wodewale beryde als a belle.
> —*Thomas of Ersseldoune*, 7 (i, 98).

> The birds sang sweet as ony bell.
> —*Sir Hugh Le Blond*, 1 (iii, 254),

and once with its doleful signification:

> Into my stomack it struck a knell.
> —*The Raid of the Reidswire*, 92 (vi, 135).

Once, too, this odd metaphor in a contest,

> And try who bears the bell away.
> —*The Duel of Wharton and Stuart*, 36 (viii, 261),

and this, where years are compared to chimes:

> And sexty yeiris cowth *ring*.
> —*The Bloody Sark*, 6 (viii, 148).

A solitary instance is

> Full many daies they *measure*.
> —*Thomas Stukeley*, 26 (vii, 308).

Twice in Barbara Allen's Cruelty do we find

> death is *printed* on his face.
> —ll. 13 and 17 (ii, 159).

Compare

> And with my teares writ in the dust my woe.
> —*Titus Andronicus*, 94 (viii, 192.)
> While with their blood, the cause they have *seald*.
> —*Undaunted Londonderry*, 49 (vii, 250).

Other products of man's ingenuity are noted once, as follows:

> His nailis wes lyk ane hellis-cruk.*
> —*The Bloody Sark*, 27 (viii, 148).
> Spots o' his dear lady's bluid,
> Shining like a lance.
> —*Lammikin*, 123-124 (iii, 311).

Once, of the product of man's skill:

> But he lay by his napkin fine,
> Was saft as ony silk.
> —*Young Waters*, 145-146 (iii, 306).

The following belong here (both again from the same poem):

> For thou must *post* to Nottingham.
> —*Robin Hood and Queen Katherine*, 15 (v, 313).
> She bids you *post* to fair London Court.
> —*Ibid.*, 45.

And, somewhat similarly:

> And he lugged her along like a pedlar's pack.
> —*The Farmer's Old Wife*, 10 (viii, 258).

---

* Hellis-crook, a hook to hang pots over the fire.

A group of figures by which a bold, saucy fellow is called a "blade," a "jolly blade," etc., perhaps demands mention in this connexion, although the derivation may be disputed. Compare the two meanings from the A. S. *blaed* (M. E. blade).

> "This is a mad blade," the butchers then said.
> —*Robin Hood and the Butcher*, 73 (v, 86).

> A jolly brisk blade, right fit for the trade.
> —*Robin Hood and Little John*, 3 (v, 216).

> Thou'rt a jolly bold blade.
> —*The Frolicksome Duke*, 59 (viii, 58).

The following are inserted for completeness of record, though they are of that special kind of extravagant simile, found only in describing some extraordinary thing, and in no other connexion. They are, therefore, of little use in proving the general ballad commonplaces.

> Her teeth was a' like tenther stakes,
> Her nose like club or mell.
> —*King Henry*, 21-22 (i, 148).

> His teeth they were like tether sticks.
> —*Kempy Kaye*, 17 (viii, 140).

> Sae they scrapt her and they scartit her,
> Like the face of an assy pan.
> —*Kempy Kaye*, 13-14 (viii, 140).

Again,

> She had a neis upon her face,
> Was like an auld pat-fit.
> —*Ibid.* (B), 31-32 (viii, 142).

(γ.) Simile and Metaphor from Man's Avocation.

Play and music and the dance are the chief sources of figures under this head, as might be expected from a rude people, as yet untrammelled by convention. Under these groupings we will draw up the figures in order. There are several instances in which a spirited contest is spoken of as a game or play, and this figure comes as near to being formulaic as any in the similes and metaphors derived from man and his habits.

> M'Intosh play'd a bonny game
> Upon the haws of Cromdale.
> —*The Haws of Cromdale*, 43-44 (vii, 236).

> But long owre a' the play wer playd.
> —*Sir Patrick Spence*, 31 (iii, 151),

and, with variations, several times again, in the same poem.

> And left the tinker *in the lurch*,
> For the great *shot* to pay.
> —*Robin Hood and The Tinker*, 71-72 (v, 233).

[Lurch (2), the name of a game (F. L. ?). The phrase "to leave in the lurch" was derived from the old game; to *lurch* is still used in playing cribbage. . . . The game is mentioned in Cottgrave. = F. *lourche*, the game called Lurche or a Lurch in game; il demoura lourche, he was left in the lurch. Cot. . . . Skeat.

Shot = reckoning, share, contribution. . . . A. S. sceotan, to shoot = that which is "shot" into the general contribution. Du. schot + Icel. skot, a shot, contribution + Germ. schoss, a shot, a scot. Cf. *scot-free*. Skeat.]

Whence the figures "in the lurch" and "shot" fairly belong to this section. For shot, compare Shakspere: "I'll to the ale-house with you presently, where for one *shot* of five pence, thou shalt have five thousand welcomes," (T. G. of V., ii, v,) and Hamlet's question concerning the players, "Who maintains 'em? How are they *escoted?*" (Ham. ii, ii); likewise, Falstaff's pun: "Though I could scape *shot free* at London, I fear the *shot* here." (Hen. IV, v, iii, 31).

Music serves once or twice for figure in the ballads:

> Where we will make our bow-strings twang,
> Musick for us most sweet.
> —*Robin Hood Rescuing Will Stutley*, 151-152 (v, 289).

> And lay my bent bow at my side,
> Which was my music sweet.
> —*Robin Hood's Death and Burial*, 69-70 (v, 311).

> The fiddle and fleet play'd ne'er sae sweet,
> As she behind her Geordie.
> —*Gight's Lady*, 137-138 (viii, 290);

and (perhaps),

> With *humming* strong liquor likewise.
> —*Robin Hood and Little John*, 118 (v, 221);

and,

> That echo made a dulefull sang,
> Thairto resounding frae the rocks.
> —*The Battle of Harlaw*, 151-152 (vii, 187).

Of the dance, we find:

> The Grahams they made their heads to dance.
> —*The Haws of Cromdale*, 55 (vii, 237);

and, satirically, of a man worsted in fight:

> He had such a chance, with a new morrice-dance,
> He never went home again.
> —*Flodden Field*, 47–48 (vii, 74).

Summary.—The figures drawn from man's life and works are again shown to be simple, but scattered. As was to be expected, the greater number of references are to agricultural pursuits and instruments, and to simple household utensils; and, from the very nature of the case, the objects referred to are as various as the poets' thoughts. No classification is possible, therefore, under this head. Under man's lighter work or avocation, we find many references to his play, and this use of "play" for battle is more nearly formulaic than anything in the present division of the subject. To conclude, we may say that in the domain of nature, and even of animal life, the figures of ballad literature run in certain grooves, which produce similar results; in the life of man the figures run in the same grooves, if you please, but the results are different. The field is wider and the figures are more "infinite in variety." All this may be but another instance of the superiority of man to his surroundings in the world, and in relation to the animal life about him.

METONYMY AND PERSONIFICATION IN THE BALLADS.

From the nature of the case, it will be seen that this essay, dealing with simile and metaphor in the ballads, is not intimately concerned with the other rhetorical figures found in the same branch of literature. Yet some idea of the old writers' uses in this respect might not, perhaps, be amiss; and it has seemed desirable to incorporate a few words on the subject of metonymy and personification, although no such care will be taken to give completeness to the list, as was attempted in the case of simile and metaphor.

It will be enough to indicate the general usage in this respect, without aiming at exactness in giving all the examples under any one head. All the important instances, however, will receive due attention.

METONYMY.

The most frequent form of this figure in the popular song is that of the use of the sign for the thing signified. We have "crown" used for kingdom; the bishop's cloak for the bishop himself, etc.

Some instances are the following:

> Had oppressed the *crowne*.
> —*Legend of King Arthur*, 63 (i, 53).

> For it never shall be said,
> That a shepherd's *hook*, at thy sturdy look,
> Will one jot be dismaied.
> —*Robin Hood and the Shepherd*, 82-84 (v, 241).

> For it becomes not your lordship's *coat*,
> To take so many lives away.
> —*Robin Hood and the Bishop*, etc., 35-36 (v, 295).

> And the warst *cloak* * of this companie.
> —*Hobie Noble*, 79 (vi, 102).

> When we attack like Highland *trews*,
> —*The Battle of Sheriff-Muir*, 72 (vii, 262).

[Trews—breeches; here—men, Scots army.]

> I will there fight *doublet* alane.
> —*Gight's Lady*, 115 (viii, 289).

> When he these lines, full fraught with *gall*.
> —*Queen Dido*, 97 (viii, 211).

Gall is used in several other places, in the same sense.

Next in frequency is the use of the abstract term for the concrete:

> There cam a schrewde arwe out of the west,
> That felde Roberts *pryde*.
> —*Robyn and Gandelyn*, 25-26 (v, 40).

> His hounds they laid her *pride*.
> —*Johnie of Breadislee*, 24 (vi, 13).

---

* Man.

> He laid the dun deer's *pride*.
> —*Johnie of Cocklesmuir*, 28 (vi, 18).
>
> With all thair *power* at thair side.
> —*The Battle of Harlaw*, 132 (vii, 186).
>
> When wars were done, I *conquest* home did bring,
> And did present my prisoners to the king.
> —*Titus Andronicus*, 17-18 (viii, 189).
>
> His lofty *courage* then did fall.
> —*Queen Dido*, 99 (viii, 211).
>
> I was not made their *scorne*.
> —*Robin Hood and the Farmer's Daughter*, 30 (v, 335).
>
> Fear not the *strength* and *frown* of Rome.
> —*Undaunted Londonderry*, 2 (vii, 248).

Another frequent usage is that of the place for its inhabitants, or of a scene for the event that took place there.

> The countre up to rout.
> —*A Little Geste, etc.*, 6 (v, 99).
>
> As England it did often say.
> —*Hobie Noble*, 6 (vi, 98),

(also personification).

> Yet that unluckie country still.
> —*King of Scots and Andrew Browne*, 13 (vii, 104);

and again, in the same poem,

> "Alas," he said, "unhappie realme."
> —*Ibid.*, 68 (vii, 106).
>
> Till ane of them the *field* sould bruik.
> —*The Battle of Harlaw*, 140 (vii, 186).

A slight variation of this form of metonymy is that where an epithet is transferred from the inhabitants of a place to the place itself, or where the epithet descriptive of the effect of the place on its inhabitants is put back upon the place itself. This is especially noted in "the merry greenwood," "merry England," etc.

> Until they came to the *merry* greenwood.
> —*Robin Hood and Guy of Gisborne*, 29 (v, 161).
>
> For all the golde in Mery Englond.
> —*A Little Geste, etc.*, 103 (v, 97).
>
> The provost of *braif* Aberdeen.
> —*The Battle of Harlaw*, 118 (vii, 185),

and various other instances.

Yet another variation is that of the epithet transferred from the effect to the cause.

> The *dizzy* crag.
> —*Kempion*, 41 (i, 140).

> The *weary* warld to wander up and down.
> —*Son Davie*, 43 (ii, 230).

> And after many *wearie* steps.
> —*The Merchant's Daughter of Bristow*, 145 (iv, 334).

> The tabull *dormounte*.
> —*The Horn of King Arthur*, 52 (i, 19).

> He heard the blows that *bauldly* ring.
> —*The Outlaw Murray*, 63 (vi, 25).

The use of the part for the whole (synecdoche), is thus represented:

> Whose notes made *sad* the listening *ear*.
> —*The Cruel Sister*, 91 (ii, 236).

> "Thou art ever in my *berde*," sayd the Abbot.
> —*A Lytell Geste of Robyn Hode*, 37 (v, 60).

The use, finally, of the material for the thing made therefrom, is particularly to be observed in the frequent employment of "tree" (in the sense of wood), for staff or spear.

> But there dyed Sir Mordred
> Presently vpon that tree.
> —*King Arthur's Death*. Folio, 193 (i, 505),

or, as Percy has emended the passage,

> Then grimmlye dyed Sir Mordered.

In "Robin Hood and the Beggar" (v, 190, ff.) *tree* is used several times for staff.

Similarly,

> But Inglond suld haif found me meil and malt.
> —*Johnie Armstrong* (B), 79 (vi, 48).

(Meil and malt = meat and drink.)

Personification.

In personification we find, in the ballads, much the usage of common life to-day. There is the assigning of reason to the elements and to the works of nature, and the picturesque presentation of abstractions like death or fortune, as concrete realities, in most cases as possessed of human form.

In the first of these two groups we find no personification so common as that of the sea.

> Beyond the *raging* sea.
> —*The Earl of Mar's Daughter*, 134 (i, 176).
>
> And *raging* grew the sea.
> —*Fragment of the Daemon Lover*, 32 (i, 303).
>
> The *raging* waves did rout.
> —*The Lowlands of Holland*, 30 (ii, 214).

Personifications of natural objects and of objects of vision are these:

> It made John sing to hear the gold ring,
> Which against the walls *cryed twang*.
> —*Little John and the Four Beggars*, 55–56 (v, 327).
>
> Thou'lt see my sword *with furie* smoke.
> —*Robin Hood and the Farmer's Daughter*, 79 (v, 338).
>
> Wae be to my cursed gowd,
> *This road to me invented*.
> —*Rob Roy*, 35–36 (vi, 205).
>
> Her bloom was like the springing flower
> That *salutes* the rosy morning.
> —*Andrew Lammie*, 5–6 (ii, 191).
>
> When the lilly leafe and the eglantine,
> Doth bud and spring with a merry *cheere*.
> —*The Noble Fisherman*, 5–6 (v, 329).

Of a ship, finally, for the customary modern "she" we find

> *Hee* is brasse within and steele without.
> —*Sir Andrew Barton*, 105 (vii, 61).

In the second division, the personification of abstract ideas, the lively representation of fortune in human form is most common.

> Till fortune *blessed* him with a *smile*,
> And shook off all his fears.
> —*The Seven Champions*, 175–176 (i, 90).
>
> In search of fortune's *smiles*.
> —*Ibid.*, 224;

where the poet, as in former instances, repeats his figure.

> If fortune once doth *smile* on mee.
> —*The Merchant's Daughter, etc.*, 131 (iv, 333).

> He blamed Dame Fortune *unkind.*
> —*Robin Hood's Chase,* 84 (v, 324).

> Fortune was pleased to give us a *frown.*
> —*The Reading Skirmish,* 14 (vii, 244).

And (again in the same poem):

> Fortune is pleased on us to *frown.*
> —*Ibid.,* 78.

> But fortune that doth often *frowne,*
> Where she before did *smile.*
> —*Fair Rosamond,* 37–38 (vii, 285).

> The skies likewise began to *scowle.*
> —*The Duchess of Suffolk,* 73 (vii, 301).

> Heaven upon their actions did *frown.*
> —*Undaunted Londonderry,* 50 (vii, 250).

Death is also personified:

> Pale Death draws near to me.
> —*Macpherson's Rant,* 6 (vi, 266).

> When death had *pierced* the tender hart.
> —*Queen Dido,* 67 (viii, 210).

Solitary instances are:

> Yet *fancy bids* thee not to fear.
> —*Queen Dido,* 63 (viii, 210).

> And did the *pleasures* of a lady *feed.*
> —*Thomas Stukeley,* 60 (vii, 309).

> In *honour's bed* he lay, man.
> —*The Battle of Tranent Muir,* 62 (vii, 171).

> And his lost *honor* must still *lye in the dust.*
> —*Sir John Suckling's Campaign,* 39 (vii, 131).

"The *wounds* of woe" (*King Lear,* 136, vii, 281); "her *fury to disarm*" (*The Spanish Virgin,* 30, iii, 361).

The personification of sorrow is also common.

> Thus was their *sorrow put to flight.*
> —*The King of France's Daughter,* 220 (iv, 224).

> *Sorrowe* wyll me *sloo.*
> —*A Little Geste,* etc., 84 (v, 120).

Similarly,

> *Hang care,* the town's our own.
> —*The King's Disguise,* 148 (v, 381).

The following are the personifications of day and night, the sun, etc.:

> This done, the *night drove on* apace.*
> —*Child Waters*, 135 (iii, 211).

> The *day it runs* full fast.
> —*Robin Hood and the Stranger*, 6 (v, 410).

> Till *Phœbus* sunk into the deep.
> —*Ibid.*, 30.

> The *day* began to *sprynge*.
> —*Robin Hood and the Monk*, 287, (v, 13).

The general nature of the metonymy and personification in the English and Scotch popular ballads will be apparent from the instances quoted. They are simple as the similes and metaphors are, yet they have a vivid picturesqueness that is all their own, and that the other figures mentioned often lack. Many of the particular cases of metonymy and personification occur several times, and acquire thereby a certain ballad propriety and authority. No attempt, however, will be made to classify them, as they are obviously somewhat out of the scope of this essay.

SUMMARY AND CONCLUSION.

If the object in writing this essay has been attained, there will no longer be any doubt as to the number and character of the figures used in the English and Scotch popular songs. Throughout the progress of the present argument, special stress has been laid on the simplicity and naturalness of the figures; they are used almost always for descriptive purposes, rather than for ornament, and are, besides, such as occur in the popular speech of all countries. It is doubtful, then, if to the popular mind such similes as *swift as the wind, like glistering gold*, and *milk-white*, had any significance other than that which belongs to all epithets of description. If a horse gallops fast, the ballad-writer says so; if he gallops very fast, he goes as

---

* Percy's, from the Folio MS. which reads:

> thiss, & itt drone now afterward
> till itt was neere the day.

(Folio, 129-130, ii, 276.)

"swift as the wind," and that is all there is to be said on the subject. We have already quoted from Motherwell to the effect that "there is no pause [in the ballads] made on the way for beautiful images or appropriate illustrations. If these come naturally and unavoidably, good and well, but there is no loitering and winding about till these should suggest themselves, . . . and rhetorical embellishments are unknown." To these remarks it may be well to add a few from another critic: "[They] throw themselves headlong into their subject, trusting to nature for that language which is at once the shortest and the most appropriate to the occasion; *spurning all far-fetched metaphors*," etc.*

Bearing this fact in mind, it will not be unprofitable, perhaps, to gather together the results of our inquiry, and tabulate the figures that seem, by their frequent use, to belong indisputably to the ballad in its purest state.

A. Under the similes and metaphors drawn from elemental nature, we find reference to the *swiftness* of the wind used too often to leave a doubt of its genuineness. The similes *still as a stone, hard as flint or stone, cold as stone*, are likewise very common; and the similes drawn from the rain and the clouds are quite numerous, particularly in the battle-songs.† The figures drawn from other elemental forces, such as thunder, hail, frost, etc., are comparatively frequent, though hardly to be classified, since no two are just the same. In the brighter aspect of nature, we find several allusions to the sunlight, *that schane byfore als the sonne so bryght*,‡ *as bright as the summer sun*, etc.

The figures drawn from plant life are more common. The metaphor by which a person is called a *flower* or a *lily* or a *rose* is known to all. Similes drawn from flowers are also common. From the life of trees no figure is so frequent as *light as leaf on lynde*, or *on tree*. The stiffness of trees as a characteristic comparison for human strength, moral or physical, is

---

* Ancient and Modern Ballad Poetry. Blackwood, 61, 622.
† Cf. Chevy Chace, The Hunting of the Cheviot, The Battle of Sheriff-Muir, etc., vol. vii.
‡ Thomas of Ersseldoune, i, 98.

also found. Other similes from tree-life are met with, but not so frequently, such as Glangary's *pith, cankerdly, cross-grained* words, etc.

In similes and metaphors of colour, nothing could be more common than *milk-white, white as snow, white as a lily, white as a swan*, etc., *red as roses, cherries, rubies*, etc., *black as a crow*, and especially, *shining like gold*, and sometimes like *silver*. Other colour-similes occur, but with the exception of *berry-brown* and *nut-brown*, they are not frequent.

Figures drawn from the mineral kingdom are rarer. Degenerate ballads like *The Damosel's Complaint, Fair Rosamond*, etc., abound in allusions to crystal—"his eyes like crystal clear,[*] etc. The best ballads are comparatively free from this simile. The metaphor *jewel* applied to persons is very common.

Figures drawn from the domain of fire are *bright as fire, glittering like the glede*, etc. The *flame of anger* and *of love* may also be frequently seen in the ballads. "The noble marquess in his heart felt *such flame*,[†] and many other similar instances.

B. Figures taken from animals and their characteristics are the similes that compare brave men to *boars, lions*, and *tigers*, and the metaphors and similes by which the terms *dog, swine*, and *ass* are contemptuously applied to human beings. The similes drawn from the lightness and agility of *deer* are also used somewhat frequently.

The figures drawn from bird-life are of one class. *Swift as a bird*, and songs as *sweet as a bird's*, are the great types of comparison. The metaphor *goss-hawk* frequently applies to man.

C. Figures from *man* are not so susceptible of classification. We find with comparative frequency references to the head and eye and to the five senses—"sought her lip to taste," etc., but the rules are not absolute.

Under the head of man in various relations of life we find the simile-adjectives *royal, princely*, etc.; sometimes expanded into "fine as a queen" and similar expressions.

---

[*] Lord Thomas of Winesberry, iv, 307.
[†] Patient Grissell, iv, 209.

Figures from man as a moral and intellectual agent refer, as we have seen, to the *madness* of courage, the *manliness* of courage, etc. There are also references to fraternal love, childhood, and other facts of life, but not so often as to degenerate into a class.

Under the works of man, the figures are too varied for classification, but all have a bearing upon navigation, agriculture, trade, and the occupations of daily life. In regard to man's sports we find the comparison of warfare to a game, and allusions to the dance and to music, but with this exception there is little to attract the notice of the reader.

It may be remarked in passing that several ideas arise in connexion with this study of ballad literature with special reference to its figures.

(*a*.) In the first place it should be noted that simile is much more frequent than metaphor, and that the similes are generally more elaborate and more novel than the metaphors. With the exception of the trite metaphors *flower*, *jewel*, *dog*, *ass*, etc., applied to human beings, there is little comparison of this sort. Such a result is, it will be observed, the opposite of the Anglo-Saxon usage, where metaphor largely predominates over the sister-figure of simile.

(β.) In the second place it should be pointed out that the figures vary according to the nature of the ballad. The figures in the poems of love and sorrow, such as Gil Morice, Fair Annet, and the rest are quite distinct from those used in the Robin Hood cycle, or from those of the Arthurian legends, and all three again are radically different in figure habit from the celebrated war-songs, such as Chevy Chace and the large body of kindred poems. What does this indicate? A different origin for the poems, either in time or place or both? There is a field of inquiry thrown open here that may lead to fruitful results.

(γ.) Again, closely related to the preceding suggestion is the fact that ballads of the artificial type—the masterpieces of the mongers—have a style of figure detestable in general, and easily detected, which sprang from the same sources as the figures in the better and simpler ballads, but which are, nevertheless, thrown in so abruptly as to take away all semblance of spontaneity from the production. A comparison of Queen Dido or Fair Rosamond or The Cruel Black with The Hunting of the Cheviot or Gil Morice or the most of the Robin Hood ballads will prove this fact beyond the shadow of a doubt.

Returning to the classification of ballad figures made a moment ago, we may apply the test to one or two of the ballads and note the result. If it be objected that all the ballads studied have contributed to the sum of these figures, and that we are, therefore, but arguing in a circle to apply to a ballad a standard that it has itself helped to form, there seems to be no counter-argument beyond the fact that each ballad is in itself so short as to make but a small proportion of the ballad literature, and its effect on that literature is therefore infinitesimal in arriving at a just conclusion on the subject; whereas, on the other hand, the sum total of these songs is sufficiently imposing to make a standard irrespective of any one or two songs that may be subjected to the proposed test. Admitting this conclusion, then, we may proceed with the investigation.

The ballad Thomas of Ersseldoune, unquestionably a popular production, has figures as follows:

> Als dose the sonne on someres daye
> That faire lady hir selfe sohe schone.
>
> And als clere golde her brydill it schone.
>
> the face
> That schane byfore als the sonne so bryght.
>
> Thomas still als stane he stude.
>
> They brittened them als they were wode.
>
> The wodewale beryde als a belle,

which are good ballad-similes, approved by more or less frequent usage. The individuality of the poet appears in these other figures:

> Als man for fude that was nere faynt;
>
> And all hir body lyke the lede.
>
> Where it was dirk as mydnyght myrke.

From our hypothesis, then, other things being equal, this proportion is sufficiently just to warrant the popular origin of the ballad.

The individuality of the poet, again, is seen in the song known as "As I Came from Walsingham," where we find *angel-like face*, and *like a queen did appear*, but where also we find

> Love liketh not the fallen fruit,
> Nor the withered tree.
> .   .   .   .
> For love is a careless child, etc.;

and

> But love is a durable fire,
> In the mind ever burning;
> Never sick, never dead, never cold,
> From itself never turning.

The subjective element in these quotations is rare in the ballads. Figures of such length are extremely uncommon. From the standpoint of figure, then, this poem does not leave the mind free from doubt.

Bishop Percy, with his passion for "polishing" the ballads, furnishes a good instance for modern criticism to deal with. Since the publication of the Folio MS. (London, 1867), we are able to tell just how far this polishing process went on, and by looking at the ballads of *King Arthur's Death* and *Sir Cauline* in the Reliques and in the Folio, we can see how much is Percy's own, and also, by applying our standard, can see how far he was justified in using the figures found in the edition of the Reliques. In Percy's published King Arthur's Death, the following figures occur:

> Oft have I reap'd the bloody feelde;

and

> Before the breakinge of the day,

which appear, so far as discovered, in no other place.

The personification, however, in the following is vouched for by other ballads:

> Nothing, my liege, save that the winds
> Now with the angry waters fought.

In "Sir Cauline" we find

> Home then pricked Syr Cauline
> As light as leafe on tree;
>
> Two goggling eyen like fire farden;

and,

> Then shee held forthe her liley-white hand;

all good ballad figures, as the learned bishop knew. The next, however, somewhat oversteps the mark:

> But ever she droopeth in her minde
> As, nipt by an ungentle winde,
> Doth some faire lillye-flower.

All these figures are Percy's, as there is no trace of them in the folio manuscript; on the whole, however, he preserved a laudable restraint in this matter, and in this as in many other cases, seems to have merited less censure than he has received.

"Fair Rosamond," the wretched production of Thomas Deloney, is full of figures that are drawn from legitimate ballad sources, yet are expressed in a style far from the true ballad style. Compare

> And from her cleare and cristall eyes
> The tears gusht out apace,
> Which like the silver pearled deaw
> Ran downe her comely face,

with this from "Fair Annet,"

> "O open, open, mother," he says,
> "O open and let me in;
> For the rain rains on my yellow hair,
> And the dew drops o'er my chin.
> And I hae my young son in my arms,
> I fear that his days are dune."

Here is the difference—easily seen, yet hard to define—between genuine poetry and the effusion of a versifier. It is the difference—without disparagement to the Roman be it said—between Homer and Virgil, between an original and a copyist; for, as in Germany the Minnesinger degenerated into the Meistersinger, so in England the balladist degenerated into the ballad-monger.

We will carry this investigation one step further. Percy, in his introduction to the beautiful ballad of Gil Morice, tells us that it ran through two editions in Scotland—the second printed in 1755. "Prefixed to them both [he adds] is an advertisement setting forth that the preservation of this poem was owing to a lady, who favoured the printers with a copy, as it was carefully collected from the mouths of old women and nurses;" and "any reader that can render it more correct or complete is desired to oblige the public with such improvements." In consequence sixteen additional verses were produced. We will now compare twelve of these with twelve of the original poem, feeling assured that no amount of criticism could better prove what the ballad style is and what decidedly it is not. The spurious verses run as follows:

> His hair was like the threeds of gold,
>   Drawne from Minerva's loome;
> His lippes like roses dropping dew,
>   His breath was a' perfume.
>
> His brow was like the mountain snae,
>   Gilt by the morning beam;
> His cheeks like living roses glow;
>   His een like azure stream.
>
> The boy was clad in robes of grene,
>   Sweete as the infant spring;
> And like the mavis on the bush,
>   He gart the vallies ring.

Such a string of figures, it may be authoritatively stated, occurs not once in any ballad that is known. This fact proves the difficulty of writing in the old ballad style; for where a modern poet with his elegant imagery would think himself most successful, he would actually fall farthest from the true ballad custom. In an article in Blackwood, LXXXVI, 24, on Modern Ballad Writers, occur the words: "It is much easier to fail in all modes of ballad composition than to succeed, and apparently most so here, where the consideration of the simplicity of the language of sorrow is apt to produce images and associations whimsical and really exaggerated."

Compare with the stilted lines quoted above the equal number from the genuine poem, and note the difference:

> The baron came to the grene wode
> Wi' mickle dule and care;
> And there he first spied Gill Morice,
> Kameing his zellow hair.
>
> "Nae wonder, nae wonder, Gill Morice,
> My lady loed thee weel;
> The fairest part of my bodie
> Is blacker than thy heel.
>
> "Zet neir the less, now, Gill Morice,
> For a' thy great beautie,
> Ze's rew the day ze eir was born,
> That head sall gae wi' me."

The true balladist, then, must be simple in his use of figures; indeed, he may omit them altogether, many of the finest ballads being wholly free from such adornment. Note *Gil Morice, Fair Annet, Sir Patrick Spens, Cospatrick*, and others, where imagery is most sparingly used, and which are yet the best and strongest of the popular songs. Figure is, in fact, an outcome of the culture of the world, and is, therefore, met with but rarely in early literatures. To come to English literature, we can see its development from the earliest times; and a short synopsis of its progression may not be amiss at this point, as helping, perhaps, to fix the time of the ballad writers.

The Anglo-Saxon epic of Beowulf contains less than twelve similes, and those of the simplest character. We will quote a few:

> Gewāt thā ofer waeg-holm winde gefȳsed
> flota fāmig-heals fugle gelīcost.
> —*Beowulf*, 217–218.

> him of eagum stōd
> līge gelīcost, leoht unfäger.
> —*Ibid.*, 727–728,

and,

> thāt hit eal gemealt īse gelīcost.
> —*Ibid.*, 1609.

Coming to Cynewulf, we note in the trained poet a vast improvement in length and force of the similes, with a marked advance in subjective beauty. The similes are still rare, but they are sometimes elaborate. One must suffice:

> . . . Feoh ǣghwām bith
> læne under lyfte, landes frætwe
> gewītath under wolcnum *winde gelīcost*
> thonne hē for hælethum, hlūd āstīgeth
> wætheth be wolcnum, wēdende fǣreth
> ond eft semninga swīge gewyrtheth
> in nēdcleofan nearwe geheathrod,
> thream forthryoced. Swā thēos world eall gewīteth
> ond ēac swā some, thē hire on wurdon.
> —*Elene*, 1270 ff.

In the *Crist*, likewise, is a very long simile, comparing life to an ocean voyage; but for practical purposes it is here omitted. Generally, however, Cynewulf's similes are shorter, and some even are as concise as those of the Beowulf; note this from the *Juliana*,

> Wēdde on gewitte swā wilde dēor.

These are better similes than we find in anything till the time of Chaucer, and, in fact, more sustained than those Chaucer himself gives us. In the barren period between the Norman Conquest and Chaucer, we glean the following similes. In the *Orm* (about 1200 A.D.) we find comparisons drawn from the sacrifices of the Jews, but little spontaneous imagery:

> & forrthi seghghth thatt Latin boc,
>   thatt thwer—utt nohht ne leghhethth,
> thatt ure Laferrd, Jesu Crist,
>   inn ure menisscnesse
> Toe thildiligh withthutenn bracc
>   thatt mann himm band withth woghhe,
> Rihht all swa summ the shep onnfoth
> Meocligh thatt mann itt clippethth.
> —*Orm*, 1182–1189.

There are many such similes in this unutterably dreary work, which will not profit in the repetition; they are preaching figures, not the natural outburst of a true poet.

Layamon's *Brut*, the production of a much finer poet (about 1205 A.D.) is almost free from comparisons. In the Hengist and Horsa episode ("Morris' Specimens of Early English") we find:

> tha wif fareth mid childe
> swa the deor wilde.
> —*Brut*, 85–86;

and,

> nes the thwong noht swithe braed;
> buten swulc a twines thraed.
> —*Ibid.*, 435–436.

In the poem *The Owl and the Nightingale*, attributed to Nicholas de Guildford (about 1250 A.D.), we meet with a few striking similes:

> Bet thughte the drem that he were
> Of harpe and pipe, than he nere
> Bet thughte that he were i-shote
> Of harpe and pipe than of throte.
> —*The Owl and the Nightingale*, 21–24.

In *King Horn* (before 1300 A.D.) we find a collection of similes that might have come from the ballads:

> Fairer his none thane he was,
> He was bright so the glas,
> He was whit so the flur,
> Rose-red was his colur.
> —*King Horn*, 13–16.

Finally, in the beautiful lyric *Spring-Time* (about 1300) occurs one striking simile that gives promise for the future:

> Ase strem that striketh stille,
> Mody meneth, so doth mo,
> Ichot ycham on of tho
> For love that likes ille.

With Chaucer we come upon the beginning of the modern art. The figures in his works, by reason of their simplicity, seem less numerous than they really are; but simile in his writings has begun to be the adornment that later poets have made it. In Chaucer, therefore, the figures are still sharp and direct, something like the ballad figures; they are, however, modern in spirit. From this point of view we will examine them, and compare them with later productions. In the first five hundred lines of the Prologue, then, we will find such similes as

>Of his port as meke as is a mayde;
>—*Prologue*, 69.

>Embrowded was he, as it were a mede
>Al ful of fresshe floures, white and rede;
>. . . . . . .
>He was as fressh as is the moneth of May.
>—*Ibid.*, 89–92;

and,

>men might his bridel heere
>Gyngle in a whistlying wynd so cleere,
>And eek as lowde as doth the chapel belle.
>—*Ibid.*, 169–171.

There is nothing more elaborate than these few instances. The general character is not unlike that of the ballads, and there is just as little of the subjective element as in the popular song.

Three instances must suffice between Chaucer and Spenser. William Dunbar, *The Thrissell and the Rois*, Stanza 8,

>The purpour sone, with tendir bemys reid,
>In orient bricht as angell did appeir,
>Throw goldin skyis putting up his heid,
>Quhois gilt tressis schone so wondir cleir.

Surrey, in *The Faithful Lover:*

>Then as the stricken deer withdraws himself alone,
>So do I seek some secret place, where I may make my moan;

and Wyatt makes the following simile a complete poem:

>From these hie hilles as when a spring doth fall,
>It trilleth downe with still and suttle course,
>Of this and that it gathers ay, and shall
>Till it have iust downflowed to stream and force,
>Then at the fote it rageth over all,
>So fareth loue, when he has tane a sourse,
>Rage is his raine, resistance vayleth none.
>The first eschue is remedy alone.

Coming to Spenser we note the steady advance, though even here the similes and metaphors are comparatively simple.

From the last stanzas of Book II, Canto xii, of *The Faerie Queene*, we pluck the following flowers of fancy:

Of the vines (Stanza 54):

> Some deepe empurpled as the Hyacine,
> Some as the Rubine laughing sweetly red,
> Some like faire Emeraudes, not yet well ripened.

A good trio of similes, by the way, in line with the ballad colour-similes.

> The whiles their snowy limbes, as through a vele, etc.

We also find *dewy face, alabaster skin, angelicall soft voices*, etc. But above all note the exquisite simile in this same canto where mortal life is compared to the rose, in seventeen as lovely verses as the English language has ever produced. This is the culmination of figure in Spenser, and with this bare notice, we leave it, to pass on to Shakspere, in whom simile reached the highest development it attained until Shelley and Tennyson made the language young again.

In Shakspere's *Venus and Adonis* (chosen for its wealth of figure) we still find no very elaborate similes, although the imagery is characterised by great freshness and beauty.

> A sudden pale,
> Like lawn being spread upon the blushing rose,
> Usurps her cheek.

> His lowering brows o'erwhelming his fair sight,
> Like misty vapours, when they blot the sky.

Shakspere, indeed, seldom goes to great length in his similes and metaphors. Compare *Hamlet's*

> this world
> Fie on't! O fie! 't is an unweeded garden,
> That grows to seed; things rank and gross in nature
> Possess it merely, etc. ;

and Capulet's

> Death lies upon her like an untimely frost
> Upon the fairest flower in all the field.

The famous verses of *Othello* (iii, 3, 440), however, are cited on the other side, as an instance of elaborate simile. The lines beginning *Like to the Pontic Sea* are too well-known to need repetition here.

Length in simile is, generally speaking, reserved for Milton, from whom we may quote one case in point:

> As when the potent rod
> Of Amram's son, in Aegypt's evil day,
> Wav'd 'round the coast, up-called a *pitchy cloud*
> Of locusts, warping on the eastern wind,
> That o'er the realm of impious Pharaoh hung,
> *Like night*, and darkened all the land of Nile:
> So numberless were these bad angels seen, etc.
> —*Paradise Lost*, i, 338–344.

This, as has been said, is the best until we reach Shelley. In Shelley, indeed, we find the perfection of figure, and the temptation is great to bring up all the noble passages from his works. Let us cite two:

> She rose like an autumnal Night that springs
>   Out of the east and follows wild and drear
> The golden Day, which on eternal wings
>   Even as a ghost abandoning a bier,
> Had left the Earth a corpse.
> —*Adonais*, xxiii.

> A pard-like spirit, beautiful and swift.
> . . . . . .
> It is a dying lamp, a falling shower,
>   A breaking billow; even whilst we speak
> Is it not broken? On the withering flower
>   The killing sun smiles brightly; on a cheek
> The life can burn in blood even while the heart may break.
> —*Ibid.*, xxxii.

In Tennyson, however, we find imagery become thought as never before, although a grain of the supernatural seems to tincture his best figures. Note these from *The Passing of Arthur*:

> an agony
> Of lamentation, like a wind that shrills
> All night in a waste land, where no one comes
> Or hath come since the making of the world.

And again:

> Then from the dawn it seemed there came, but faint
> As from beyond the limit of the world,

> Like the last echo born of a great cry,
> Sounds as if some fair city were one voice
> Around a king returning from his wars.

There will be little difficulty in seeing in these examples the progression of English simile and metaphor toward nobility and grandeur of thought and language. The ballads, perhaps, were in many cases composed before the full dawn of simile and metaphor, and tradition may have preserved the old figures in them without change or innovation. This is, possibly, a plea for the antiquity of the ballads, which it is left for future essayists to prove.

It may be well to close this paper with a comparison of one or two modern ballads, in their choice of figure, with the standard we have found in the old ballads.

Coleridge, for instance, in *The Rime of the Ancient Mariner*, uses many similes that have warrant in the models of popular song. Some of these are *And listens like a three years' child, Red as a rose is she, the snowy clifts, Her locks were yellow as gold, Like April hoar-frost spread, golden fire, The harbour bay was clear as glass*, etc. But the greater number are too fine for ballad writing. One—and that of the best—will suffice for comparative quotation:

> And see those sails,
> How thin they are and sere.
> I never saw aught like to them
> Unless perchance it were
>
> Brown skeletons of leaves that lag
> My forest brook along;
> When the ivy-tod is heavy with snow,
> And the owlet whoops to the wolf below,
> That eats the she-wolf's young.

Scott, on the other hand, the best of all the modern ballad writers, in his *Eve of St. John*, uses but two similes:

> Then changed, I trow, was that bold Baron's brow,
> From the dark to the *blood-red* high,

and

> For it scorched like a fiery brand;

both good ballad figures. Such restraint is remarkable, and shows how deep must have been Scott's appreciation and understanding of the ballad style. In *The Battle of Beal'an Duine*, likewise, Scott uses certain variations of true ballad figures that are neat and extremely ingenious. Further investigation in this field, however, seems unnecessary, as the subject has been exhausted by many critics and poets of note from Percy down to Algernon Charles Swinburne.

The ballad, notwithstanding, is dead; the story paper has taken its place. Those songs that we have may serve to quicken and inspire many poets yet to come; but the wise bard will not force imitation of them to too great length. The ballad-writer has lived and had his day, and the ballad-monger is no substitute for him. Poetry has many notes, and that of the ballad carries far, and wakens chords in many hearts; but the note is faint and dying, and cannot be reproduced by future writers. The old balladists exhausted the field, and the modern poet must deal with the facts of life as he sees them about him.

> So perish the old Gods !
> But out of the Sea of Time
> Rises a new Land of Song,
> Fairer than the Old.
> Over the meadows green
> Walk the young Bards and sing.

APPENDIX.

EDUCATIONAL INSTITUTIONS ATTENDED BY THE AUTHOR.

1874-1879. Grammar School, Newburgh, N. Y.
1879-1883. The Newburgh Academy.
1884-1885. Siglar Preparatory School, Newburgh.
1885-1892. Columbia College, New York City.

DEGREES AND HONOURS CONFERRED UPON THE AUTHOR.

1889. A.B., Columbia College.
     Honours in Greek, Latin, English, and Philosophy, Columbia College.
1889-1891. Prize Fellow in Letters, Assistant in Latin; Columbia College.
1890. A.M., Columbia College.
1891-1892. University Fellow in English, Columbia College.

www.ingramcontent.com/pod-product-compliance
Lightning Source LLC
Chambersburg PA
CBHW020148170426
43199CB00010B/941